DAVID ALLAN BROWN

ANY SERVICE MEMBER

MAIL FROM DESERT STORM ANSWERED

OscMay Publishing

ISBN: 978-0-578-88707-4
Imprint: Independently published

Cover Design by Matthew Morse
Printed in the United States of America

DEDICATION

Dedicated to the many patriots that selflessly took the time to write soldiers serving during Operation Desert Shield and later, Operation Desert Storm. Your correspondence provided the support and oftentimes, inspired the motivation for soldiers to push through the fear and exhaustion. Ultimately, each of you served as "home-based" soldiers that inspired victory in the Persian Gulf. Thank you!

CONTENTS

*"You never know when a moment and a few sincere words
can have an impact on a life."*

— ZIG ZIGLAR

*"The way we communicate with others and with ourselves
ultimately determines the quality of our lives."*

— ANTHONY ROBBINS

PROLOGUE

At nights, I would locate a spot outside of the perimeter, lay in the sand and gaze into the sky, sometimes coaxed to sleep by the peace taking place above the battlefield. Yes, it was a very careless thing to do, but well worth the risk. The desert has the ability to project or provide a false image that the stars are within reach; large and bright, sort of like looking at a cityscape at night. The lights of the skyscrapers demand all the attention while none of the activities taking place within and around are visible. The hypnotic tendency of the sparkling heavens delivers a sense of peace and a harmony that momentarily dwarfs any earthly activities, and if only for that moment, allows a person to forget even the horror of war. Very few images or activities can duplicate the feeling I felt as I on many occasions laid in the sand searching the universe for the Little and Big Dipper, the North Star, Rigel, and Vega.

The only other event that delivered a similar harmonious feeling was when a shipment of mail arrived and was distributed amongst the troops. Mail from family and friends always lightened the moment and brought a joy to the often-exhausted soldiers. At the same time, letters from unknown people, letters addressed to "Any Service Member," brought just as much, if not more, happiness to each and every soldier's life these "mystery" writers touched. Personally, each and every letter I was fortunate enough to receive, refreshed my spirit and permitted me to push through the fatigue and fear.

Many of the authors of these letters openly solicited a reply while others never asked but were deserving of a reply just as well. The people that took the time out of their day to write miscellaneous soldiers unknowingly became the "Twelfth Man" on the battlefield. Their words served as a motivating force, a spiritual catalyst that directly lead to victory during Desert Storm.

I did manage to reply to many of the letters received at that time, but unfortunately, I was unable to reply to most and due to the passage of time, I am not sure which letters I replied to and which ones I did not. This novel serves as a historical archive of the many letters, the names, and people that touched my life during Desert Storm as well as functions as a platform to present each writer by name, provide their state of residence at that time, and allow me to provide a well-deserved reply to each and every patriot that took the time to do their part in support of Operation Desert Storm. Some of the replies I wrote during the war with the intentions of mailing, but for one reason or another, they were never mailed. Other replies are written from the perspective of Staff Sergeant Brown (Me) as if still in the Persian Gulf during Desert Storm. I can only speak of those that directly impacted me through their writing, but I pay homage to the hundreds of thousands of others who took the time to patri- otically reach out in support of the troops. I hope you find your names among those in the letters that follow. I'm deeply indebted and thankful to all of you and secretly hope some of those who chose to send "Any Service Member" mail find copies of their letters enclosed, are able to read my reply, and ultimately, hope this platform serves as a springboard for some to reach out and share their lives with me once again.

CHAPTER 1

CORRESPONDENCE FROM SCHOOLS AND COLLEGES

Since my departure from the military many years ago, I have worked in many facets of the business world, but eventually decided on a career as a teacher. While in the Army, I once served as a Training NCO and thoroughly enjoyed teaching tactics, skill qualification tasks, and marksmanship. My experience teaching in the military convinced me that I wanted to be an educator. Teaching is a career that at times is under-recognized, but there are many other career paths that unfortunately, do not get the recognition they deserve such as police officers, and firefighters. At the same time, I argue, especially in the Covid-19 era that we now live in, many other under celebrated employments include food service workers, nurses, construction workers, among others who deserve our deepest appreciation (Sorry if I missed any careers and trades). Out of all of these various trades, many school staff members, students, and schools as a whole supported troops through their writing during Desert Storm.

Recently, I discovered a box that I long forgot existed. When I cracked the box open I was excited to discover all of the letters I received while serving in the Persian Gulf. A large envelope fell at my feet addressed as follows:

Mrs. Dixon's Class
Jesse Wharton Elementary School
Greensboro, North Carolina 27405

Each student in her class made a beautiful heart shaped card with a personal message on each. As much as I would have like to provide images of each and every card, due to the constraints of this publication, I have uploaded eight of the more "expressive" messages not because they were any more important than the rest, but because after so many years not all were readable. The students that contributed are identified below (Unfortunately, most last names were not provided):

1. Bryant
2. Haj
3. Billy
4. John Biles
5. Sheldon
6. Terrick
7. Jason Hutcherson
8. Michael
9. Rakisha
10. Cristin
11. Jason Lucas
12. Julius
13. Madaka
14. Chequilla
15. Natasha
16. Kristle
17. Jennifer
18. Sarah

Dear Mrs. Dixon and Students,

Your cards were very impactful and were shared by many of my friends. You all brought a great amount of joy as well as a reason to finish things up in a timely manner and return home. I thank you Mrs. Dixon for taking the time to allow your students to send their very spirited and uplifting messages. If I could have at the time, I would have traveled to North Carolina to meet and personally thank each one of you. I still hold hopes of one day meeting each of you.

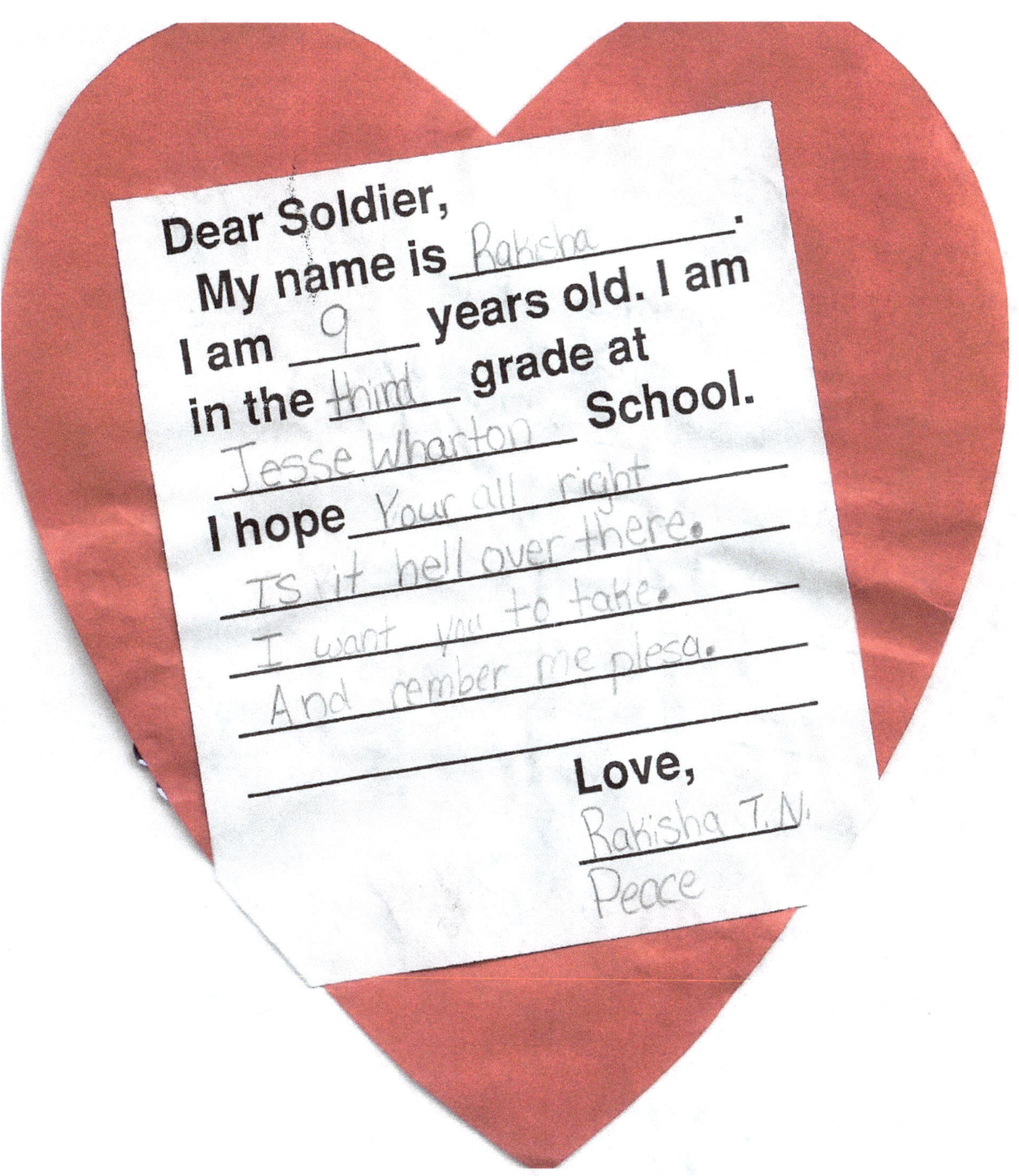

Dear Rakisha,

I especially loved your message. Yes, at times it seemed like what I would picture hell to be. I do remember your message. Many of my squad members read your card and we laughed, and at the same time, deeply appreciated your thoughts. I hope this message finds you well! Thank you!

— Staff Sergeant David Brown

Dear Jason,

It was another busy day in the desert. The temperatures are around 110 every day and the sandstorms are blinding. We all did our very best. Thank you for the awesome card!

SSG. David Brown

Dear Terrick,

I did live, and I am okay. I don't believe I was the person you intended this card to go to, but I appreciated it probably as much as the person who you intended it to go to would have. Thanks!

SSG. Brown

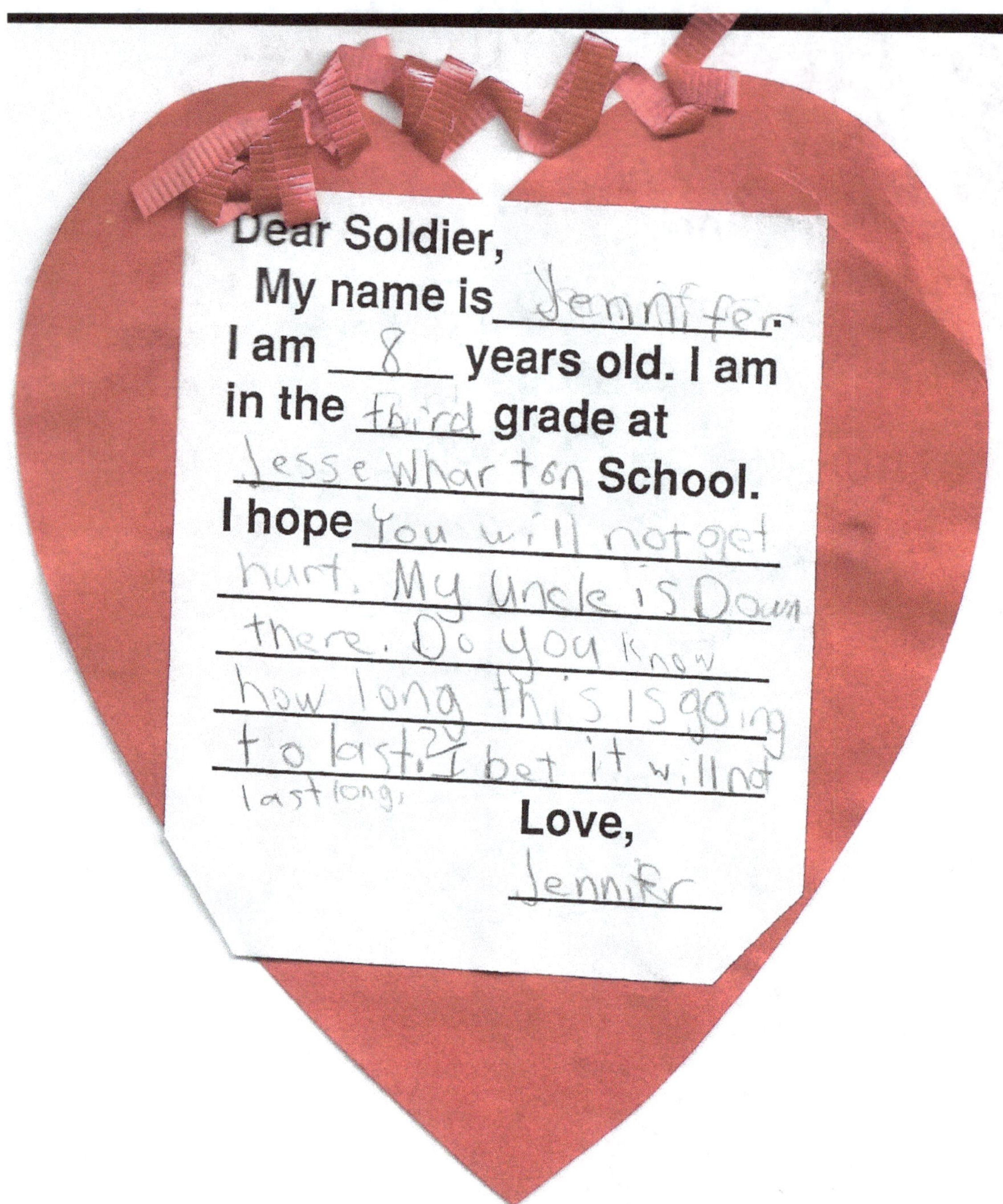

Dear Jennifer,

I am doing my best to not get hurt. We are taking care of each other, so things should be fine. Your uncle will be fine too---just don't worry. I have no idea how long we will be here, but hopefully not more than a few months. Thanks for the card!

Your Friend,

SSG. David Brown

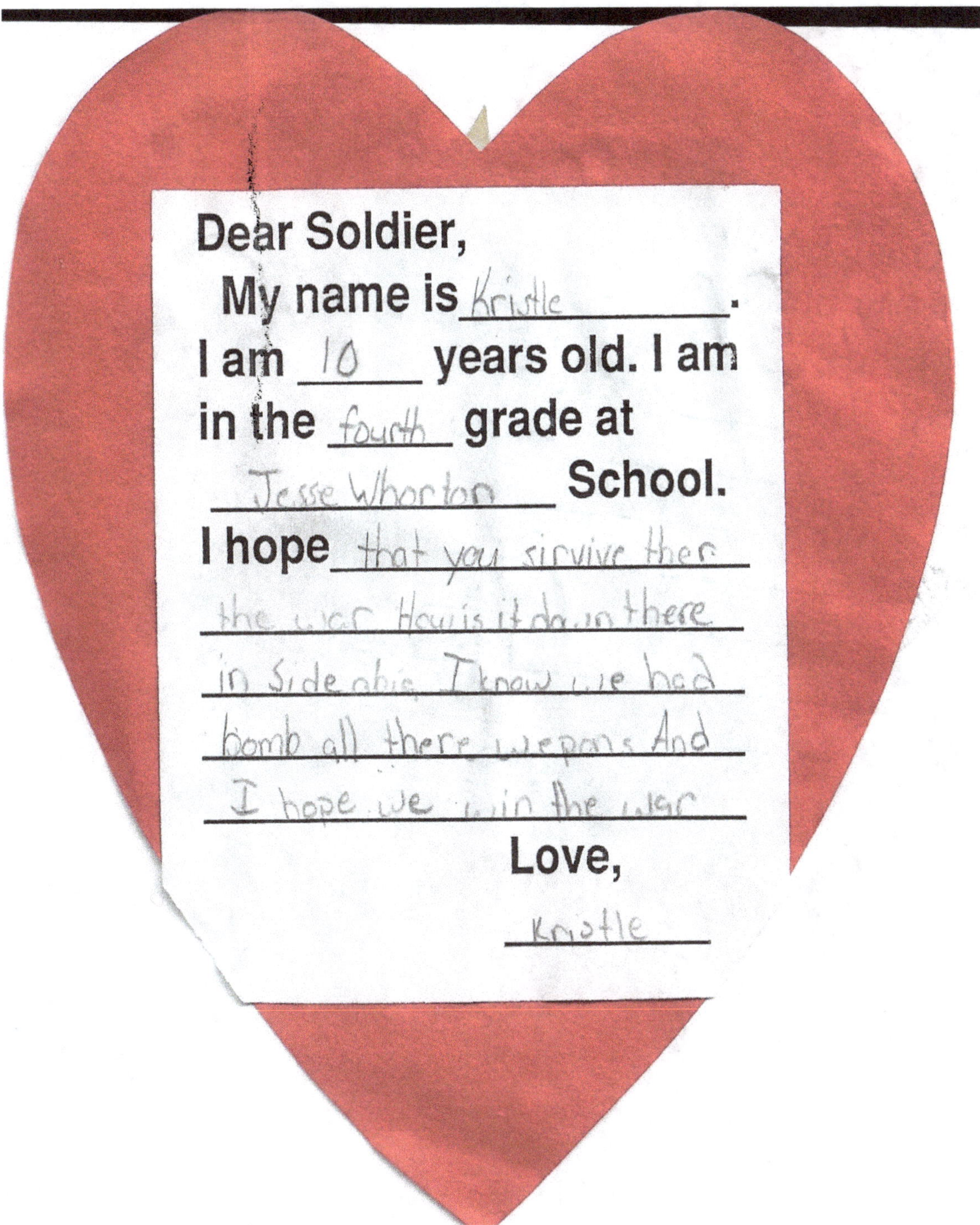

Dear Kristie,

Thanks for hoping I survive. I kind of hope I do too! It is very hot and dry in Saudi Arabia. There aren't many trees and there is lots of sand! Yes, we did bomb their weapons, but we had to in order to make sure our people weren't hurt. I think it is a sure thing that we will win this war, so don't worry. When you begin to worry, just remember your parents are there for you and also, we, the U.S. Army have your back! Thanks for writing.

SSG. David Brown

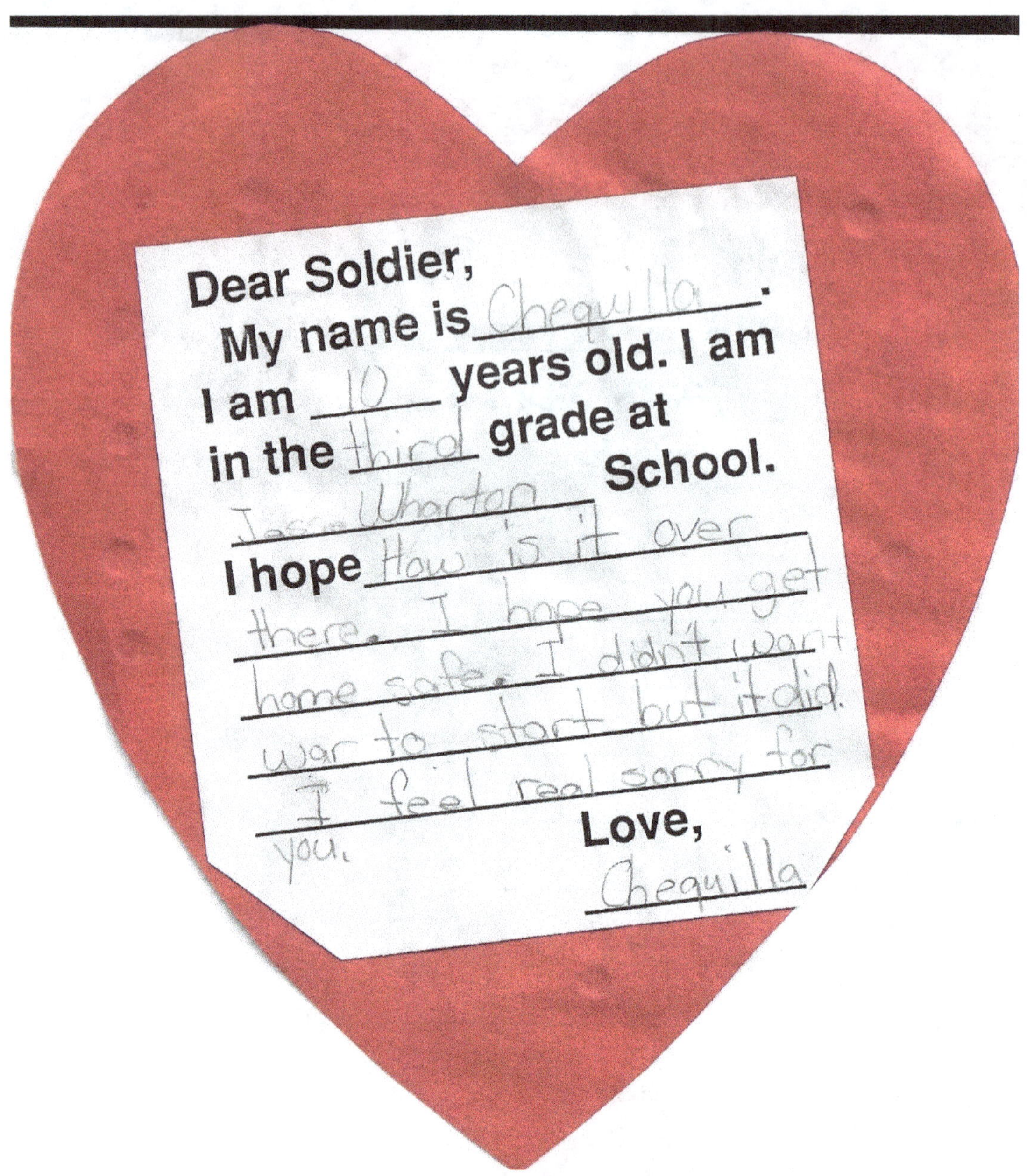

Dear Chequilla,

You have a very unique and pretty name. You ask, "How is it over there?" Well it is different. The buildings and homes are way different than ours, there is not too much vegetation like grass and trees, and there is more sand than you will ever see in a lifetime. Like you, I didn't want the war to start. War is a very bad thing, but; unfortunately, sometimes necessary to help others. You don't have to feel sorry for me since I joined the Army for a reason and knew there was a chance that we would one day go to war. Thanks for the nice card and for writing.

Your Friend,
SSG. David Brown

Dear Madaka,

I am doing Okay. Thanks for asking. If I met you and got to know you, I am sure we would be good friends. Don't miss me too much since I don't plan on being here too long. In the meantime, take care of yourself and work hard in school! Thanks for writing!

SSG. David Brown

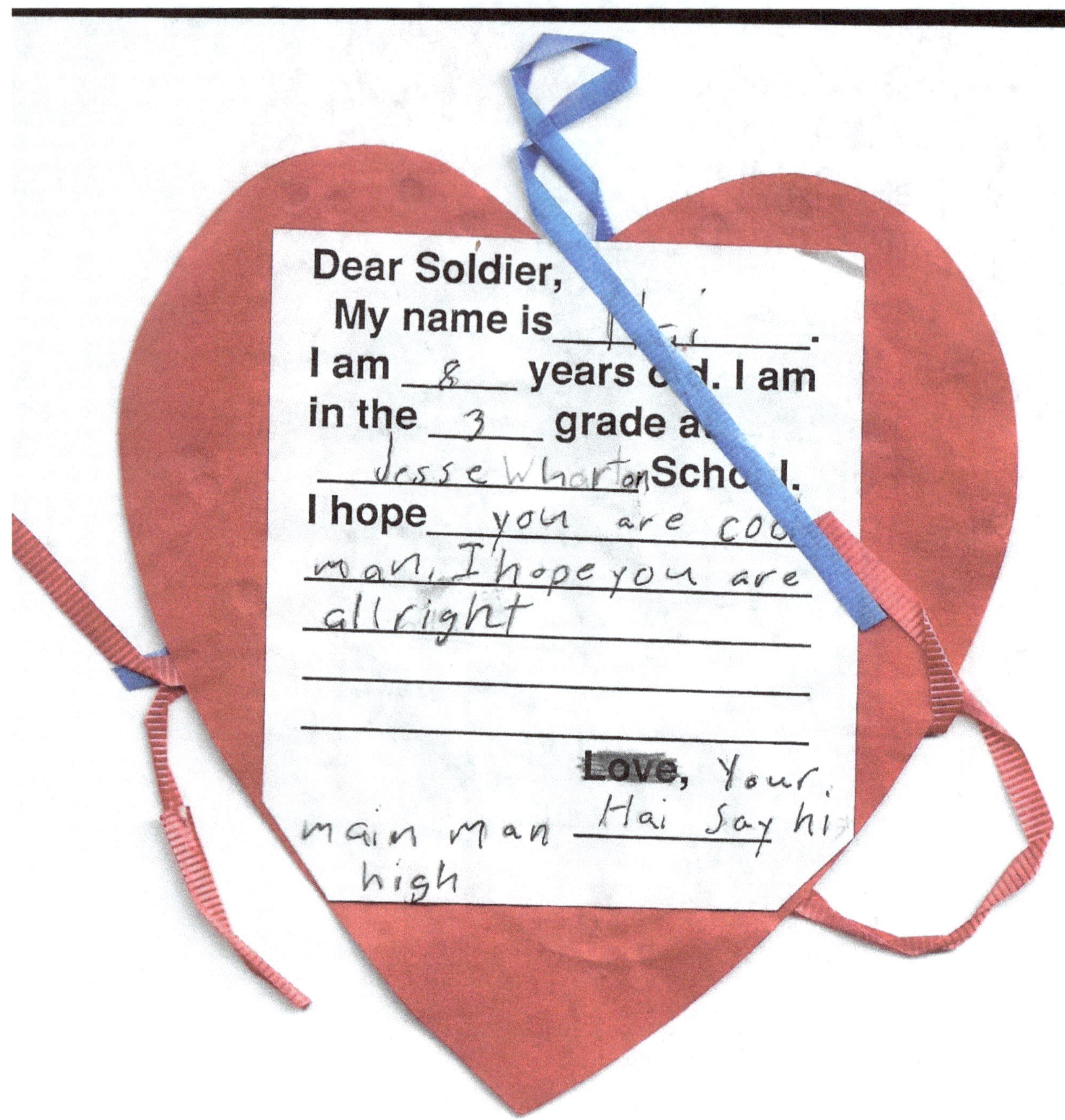

Dear Hai,

Thanks for saying I am cool---I really don't know if I am though, after all, my friends call me Professor---Does that sound cool? I am alright and doing well. Just a bit tired and worn out from the heat. I am not sure if you were calling me your "Main man," but I am honored if you did. Hello to you from Iraq, Saudi Arabia, and Kuwait.

Your Friend,
SSG. David Brown

The letter that follows is one that I especially regret not replying to. Cecily Mauch was so open and curious while at the same time, compassionate. I planned on writing, but we were in the midst of some very intense situations at the time. She also wrote me a second time. I will share that letter later. My response is below---I wish I could have met you Cecily!

Cecily Mauch
Glendale, AZ 85301

1/24/91
Glendale
~~Phoenix,~~ AZ

U.S. Airman, or ~~U~~U.S. Soldier

Sorry so formal, but because I don't know you I wasn't really sure how to start. I guess I should introduce myself. My name is Cecily Mauch (I know it's hard to pronounce). I'm 18 years old + a senior at Glendale High School in ~~Phoenix,~~ Glendale AZ. I've never written a letter to someone I didn't know so if this seems stupid, please bear with me.

I know that what we hear on the news isn't always exact to what is going on over there. If it is possable, + you get the chance or feel like writing back could you please send a little word on how things are going. I would really appreciate it.

I do realize that what is going on is some times confidental but I want you to know that I support you all 100%. I know you're doing it because you were trained for this + what you are part of our country's military for + I think it's great.

This letter must sound really egocentric with all the "I"s in it, But the only person I really know anything about right now is me. I hope that doesn't sound stuck-up. Because I'm not, I don't think.

I could ask you a few questions though. Where are you from? If you don't mind my asking, what is your name? Could you describe yourself for me? I know these are personal questions, so you don't have to answer if you don't want to. I know it's sometimes hard to ~~be~~ tell people you don't know things about yourself. If it would help I'll tell a little more about myself.

I'm 5'3" with brown hair + hazal eyes. When I graduate this year I'm going to go to Oklahoma Christian University. I went to a Christian school for 8yrs + really liked it there, so I thought this college would be nice too. I'm studying to be an adolesent or teen counselor. It may not pay much but the reward I feel will be ~~faithful~~ fulfilling. I'm not really sure what else to say so I guess I'll say good-bye. If you want to or get the time you can ~~write~~ write me back.

sincerly,
Cecily Mauch.
A devout supporter.

Dear Cecily,

By now you have graduated from Glendale High School long ago. Your letter in no way seemed egocentric and in fact, was just the opposite. To answer some of your questions, I graduated High School in Pennsylvania, my name is David Brown, I am about 5'6 with brown hair (Lots of gray now), and I also have hazel eyes. I hope you were able to attend Oklahoma Christian University and that you have graduated and have a career by now. Hopefully, you are the counselor you wanted to be. Thanks for taking the time to ask your questions and for taking time to write. I hope this reply finds you well. Take care!

SSG. David Brown

Dear Carole,

I received thirty-eight letters from the Aubrey Independent School District. The students that wrote attended either Aubrey Middle School, Aubrey Jr. High, or Aubrey High School. Thank you Mrs. Carole Hunt for taking the time to have your students write. I remember spending many days reading through them. I enoyed them all. Thank you!

I received letters from the following students from the Aubrey School District

1. Tonya Redfern
2. Alissa McDonald
3. Amanda Busby
4. Craig Arrington
5. Robert Bridgman
6. Cristal Rice
7. Alfred Kuzov
8. Steven Gruenwold
9. Abigail Fretwell
10. Misty Cardwell
11. Kevin Woopley

12. Jessica Jacobs
13. Dee Ann Mullen
14. Megan McIntire
15. Jimmy Hodges
16. Billy Breon
17. Patsi Starr
18. Stacy Thomas
19. Tiffany Reynolds
20. Bobb Sparks
21. Michelle Blaud (Randi)
22. Patrick C. Nunley

23. Tiffany Reynolds
24. Trina Brockett
25. Gavino Lopez
26. Shaun Davidson
27. Kinda Griswold
28. Stacy Hodges
29. Tonya Redfearn
30. Misty Redfearn
31. Brandy Milroy
32. Delinda Musgrave (Dee Dee)

33. Ian Baker
34. Jon Anderson
35. Bubba Bland
36. Monica Gilluland
37. Brandy Hurder
38. Jason Blalock

Thank all of you for your thoughtful and entertaining letters

1/17/91

Dear Soldier(s),

I hope the war is over soon so you can come home soon to your family. Over here in (America) people are protesting and saying "No more war." Why can't people get it it through their thick heads that the war has already begun and theres nothing they can do about it but stick together as a nation and back you guys up. You guys are the people who have the guts to go out there and protect our country (a wonderful country at that), Besides you guys are (Americans) so while your over there show them Iraqis what (Americans) are made of. I am an 11 year old boy,

- Your Fellow (American),

Kevin Woosley

P.S.
Stomp on Hussien like hes is a bug,
(Which he is)

Dear Kevin,

I didn't know anything about the protests you mention. In fact, we didn't see any news nearly the whole time we were in the Persian Gulf region. I wish people back then could have gotten it, "Through their thick heads," like you mention and just accepted that the war was taking place, but as a nation we will never all agree unanimously on anything. The main thing is that we at least communicate and maintain an open and tolerant discussion. We did our best to "Show those Iraqis what Americans are made of." I hope we made you proud.

Sincerely,

SSG. David Brown

Dear Soldier,
My name is Delinda. You can call me Dee Dee (That's my nickname), I hope your okay, If your not Get OKAY SOON.
I hope this war doesn't last long! I really don't understand why or what this war is about.
I'm in 6th grade, In history we just got through learning about the Middle East. We have been watching the news alot in school, We also Isson to radices.
Alot of people in 6th grade worry about all of yall people in Saudi Arabia. I bet its scary! I'm scared!
I wish you and all of you all could come home soon! I'm not the only one wishing this.
What is the desert like? I sometimes wonder. What are you going through, is another thing I wonder.
Everybody is asking questions to teachers and people that they can't answer. I even have been but I just realized that.
Well, I hope you come home soon!
Your unknown friend,
Delinda Musgrove (Dee Dee)

Dear Dee Dee,

I like your nickname, but Delinda is really pretty too! I am okay now that I am home and have been for many years. I appreciate that you worried about us and thanks for wishing all of us well. To answer your question, the desert is extremely hot, very dusty, with lots of bugs to include huge scorpions. By now, you have the answers you were looking for regarding the war. I am sorry that you were scared, but things ended quickly, and you are safe. I hope to hear back from you one day. I would love to hear how your life is going. Thanks for taking the time to write and for your kind thoughts.

Your friend,

SSG. David Brown

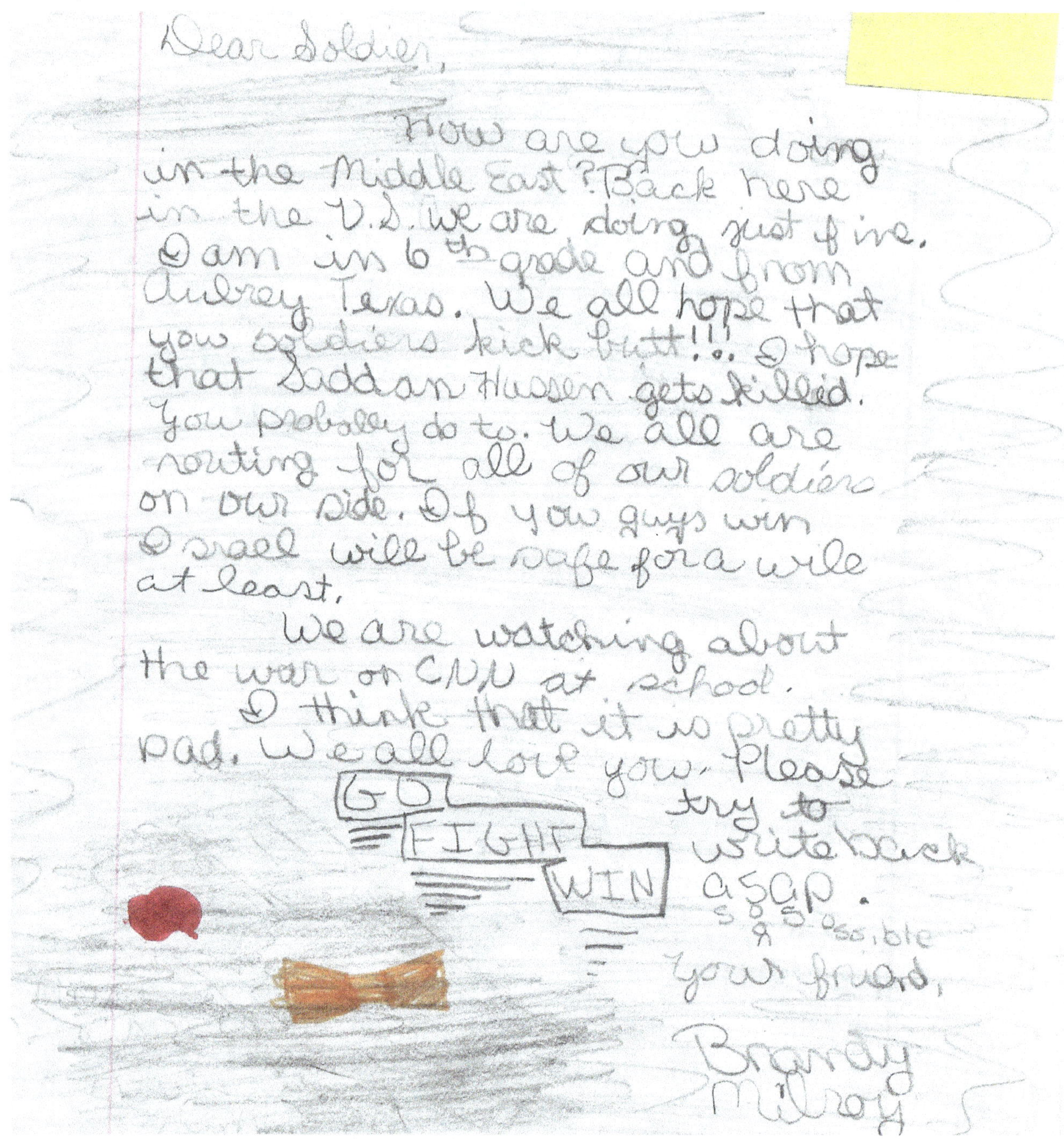

Dear Brandy,

Thank you for the nice letter. Sorry it took me so long to get back with you. We tried to "Kick [as much] butt" as possible while in the Middle East. Thanks for rooting for all of us. We will do our very best---I promise! You are right about Israel being safe now. I liked your cheer---"Go-Fight-Win." Take care of yourself!

Your Friend,

SSG. David Brown

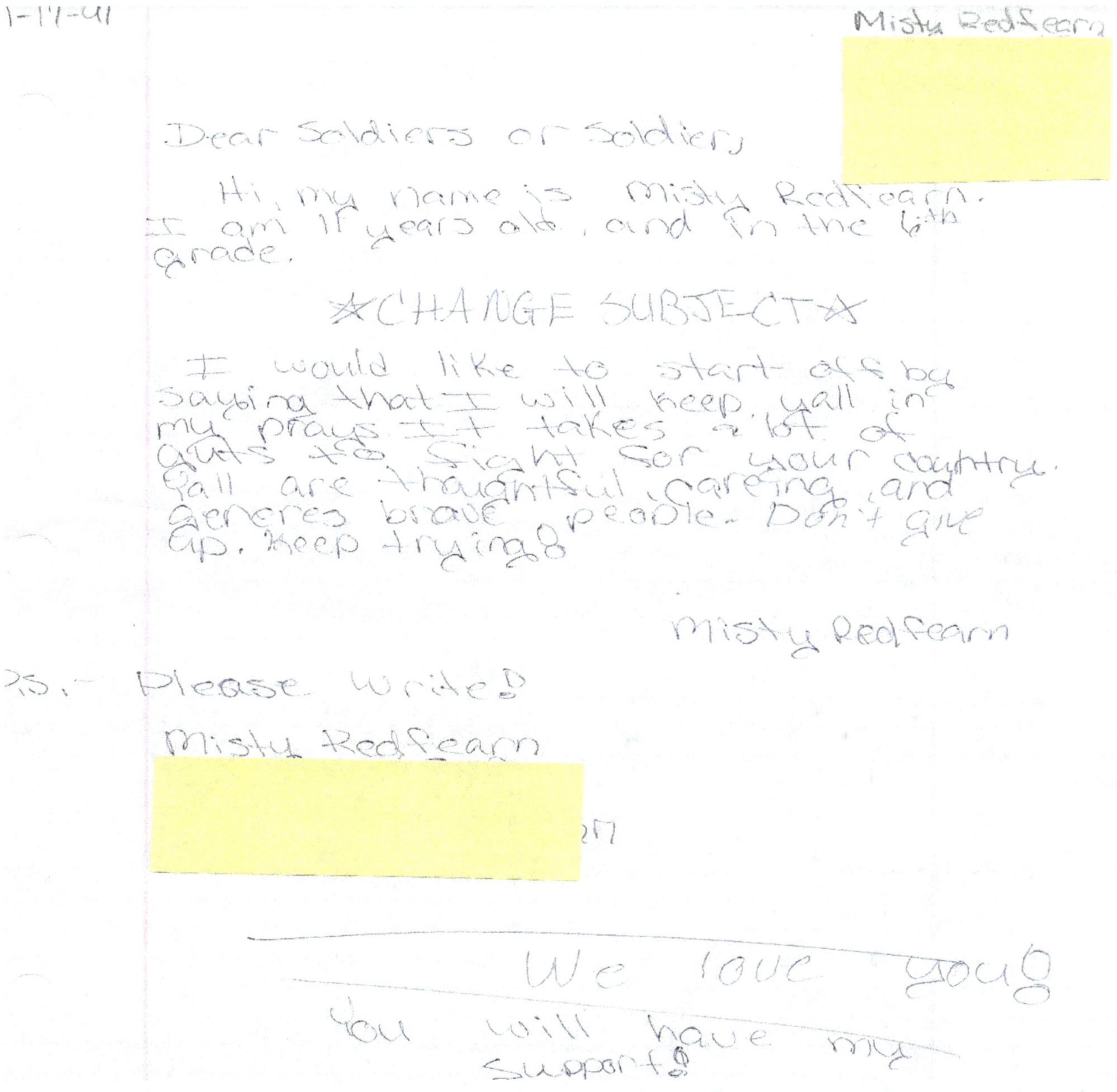

1-17-41

Misty Redfearn
[redacted]

Dear Soldiers or Soldier,

Hi, my name is Misty Redfearn. I am 11 years old, and in the 6th grade.

CHANGE SUBJECT

I would like to start off by saying that I will keep yall in my prays It takes a lot of guts to fight for your country. Yall are thoughtful, careing, and generes brave people. Don't give up. Keep trying!

Misty Redfearn

PS. Please write!
Misty Redfearn
[redacted]

We love you!

You will have my support!

Dear Misty,

I hope you are doing well. Thanks for your letter. I read it many times. Thanks for keeping us in your prayers. I promise not to give up and to keep trying no matter what. Thanks for your support. Good luck at school. Do your best!

SSG. David Brown

Dear Soldier,

Hey dude what's going on, I know you're probably in the middle of war right now but I'm sure you're going to be fine when it's all over.

When you're here, in America you have your own family but when you're over there we your country are your family.

Right now I'm watching CNN live about the war. Well I heard that you had a visit from Bob Hope.

My name is Jon Anderson I'm 11 years old in sixth grade and live in Aubrey Texas.

If you get close enough to Saddam Husien be sure + punch him in the nose and tell him "that was from Jon Anderson back home."

Well I'd better let you get back to kicking But and getting victory for us back here. When you get out of the war please write me back.

Look on the back → for I'm PROUD of YOU!

Dear Jon,

Thanks for the beautiful picture of the U.S. flag you put on the back of this letter. I wasn't exactly in the middle of war when I read your letter, but was resting up after. I like your idea of how, "the country is [our] family" while I/we are over here. The idea makes me feel cared for and missed. I didn't get close enough to Saddam to punch him. As a matter of fact, I didn't see him at all, just a lot of his soldiers. I will try to punch one of them in the nose for you! Bob Hope may have visited, but he doesn't travel to the front lines, so I wasn't lucky enough to see him. Thanks for being proud of us. Good luck in school. Take care!

Your friend,

SSG. David Brown

Jan. 17, 1991

Dear Soldier,

I am writing to you from Aubrey, Tx. All of America is worried sick about your guys and gals. I have a couple cousins over in the navy. When I was watching T.V. last night I heard that one of the ships launched alot of Tomahawk cruise missles. My opinion was not to have war, but since we have started bombing we can't stop it. All I can say is get this war over with and come home.

Your American Friend,
Steven Gruenwald
from Aubrey M/High School

P.S. Kick Saddam Hussein's "big" foreign but.

Dear Steven,

It is nice to hear that people are worried about us, but I wish they wouldn't. We are doing the job we were trained for and we are glad that our families (at least most of them) are home and safe while we wrap this war up. I wish I could have met your two cousins in the Navy, but that is very doubtful; since they are on a ship while we are deep in the desert of Iraq. I bet they are very brave and doing a fantastic job lobbing those Tomahawk missiles to their intended targets. I like your opinion of war. After seeing the unbridled violence that is war, I believe it should be avoided at all costs if possible. We will try to get this war over with as quick as we can. Thanks for writing.

Sincerely,

SSG. David Brown

Patrick C. Nunley
Jan. 17, 1991

Dear souldier,
    I'm from Aubrey, Texas. I am in the sixth grade at Aubrey high school. Thank you for volunteering to ~~defend~~ defend our country. I have heard about the start of the war on television. I am thankful only two planes were shot down in all. I have heard the air attack, the day of the start of the war, was good. I hope this does not become like Vietnam. Around the U. S. there has been many protests for peace. Also there has been terrorist bomb threats. I hope there are no more casualties, though I know there will be. Many families have been attending church, and praying for their lovedones. Turkey is also helping against Iraq. I am worried about my greataunt in Saudi Arabia.

                    Sincerely,
                    Patrick C. Nunley

Dear Patrick,

Hello from Iraq! I have never been to Aubrey, Texas. Is it nice there? You were watching a historical event when you watched footage on the beginning of the war. I was anxiously waiting for the war to begin in order to get things over with. The unit I am in waited on the border for days for the order to go into Iraq. Artillery fired for days straight while fighter jets bombed Iraqi troops repeatedly. I would have hated to have been them. The air war has gone very well and has provided us an advantage that Saddam's troops cannot overcome. The winner of this war was decided before it even began---Iraq will lose and their defeat should happen fairly quickly. This war is nothing like Vietnam and shouldn't be nearly as deadly.

I hate to hear about the protests, but the right to express oneself is part of what makes America a great country. Unfortunately, there will always be whackos that threaten bombing facilities. One good thing that comes from this war is that it is bringing our country and the world together. It's funny how war has the ability to unite so many people.

Well, thanks for writing. I enjoyed your thoughts. I bet your aunt will be fine in Saudi Arabia.

Take care!

SSG. David Brown

Kinda Griswold

age 12 grade 6
Aubrey, Texas 76227

Dear solider,

Hi!! My name is Kinda Griswold. How are you? I okay. I'm scared to death because of the war. My friends think that the war will only last a few weeks. I keep telling them it will last longer though. I think that the only thing this war is about money and greed. I don't know anyone over in the Middle East, but I still fear for your lives. Prices are going up on everything. I wish this war would have never started. I bet you do to. My gradma is a nurse and one of her friends from the hospital was shipped to Germany to care for the hurt soliders. Right now at school we are watching a

special about the war. I am
very scared because I
don't want anyone to die.
My little sister doesn't sleep
at night ~~once~~ anymore because
she is afraid someone is
going to kill her. Alot of
people are saying that Saddam
Huissen wants to take
over the entire world, and
that he is also a mad
man. Did you see Bob Hope
at Christmas? They showed a
television spiecal on it. Alot of
famous people were there.
Well I have nothing more to
say except that, Good Luck
and May God bless you

Your friend,

Kinda Griswold

Dear Kinda Griswold,

Well, hello again. You are quite the writer. You mention that you are "Scared to death because of the war," but you do not need to be. We are well-trained and have huge advantages militarily. You are safe there in America. I believe you are right in your idea that war is about money and greed because that is so often true; however, while Desert Storm may have something to do with money, I believe the important part is that we are helping a country and its people rid themselves of a very evil person and his army.

I didn't know that prices were going up on things. What types of products are increasing in price? Just curious. Most people agree with you when you wish the war would never have happened. Hopefully things will end soon. Nobody really wants war since it results in so much death and harm.

That is brave of your grandmother's friend to go to Germany and help injured soldiers. Do you know where she will be in Germany? I have lived the last 2-1/2 years there. I think it is neat that your teacher is letting you watch footage on the war. One day everything you are watching and everything going on here in the Persian Gulf will be in the history books.

I am sorry about your sister being so scared she can't sleep. Just explain to her that she is safe in America. We will handle things here. I think that you are right again when you said Saddam wants to take over the world. I imagine he probably would if he was able, but that will not happen on our watch.

No, I did not get to see Bob Hope's show. Those shows normally take place at safe places. My unit is deep in Iraq on the frontlines. I would have loved to have seen him though. While I am disappointed about not seeing him, your letter was entertaining enough for me! Thanks for writing. I hope to hear from you again.

Your Friend,

SSG. David Brown

Dear Totally Cool Soldier,

How's it going, Hope things aren't to tuff and I really hope you can kick Hussein's butt! Well if you really want to know my name is Ian Baker. I'm in 6th grade. I live in Aubrey, Teaxas, I hope you don't have to much stress. Over here we call Hussein "Insain" Hussein. If you do get a hold of Hussein, please kick him just for me, Dude. Man I really hate this war. I gotta go to lunch, Hope we win!

your friend,
soldier Ian Baker

1,000 LBS

U.S.

Hussein

Dear Ian,

Things are going pretty good here---everything considered. It's not so tough here. It is very hot and dusty with tons of flies. We are working very hard to "Kick Hussein's Butt." There is some stress depending on what's going on around us, but not too bad most of the time.

I think not just you, but many people are calling Saddam "Insane" at this point. He definitely has some serious issues. I doubt I will see Saddam himself---so, no I can't kick him for you. I do see many of his soldiers and we have taken a few prisoner, but I don't want to kick them either. They have been through enough. I hope all of this ends too.

Well Ian, I've got to go. Thanks for the letter and the cool picture. I especially like the 1,000 pound weight over Saddam's (The Bug's) head. Nice!

Take care of yourself!

SSG. David Brown

Tiffany Reynolds

Aubrey Tx 76227

Dear, Soldier,
HI! How are you down (over) there? Fine here in Texas so far. Have you fought any or are you just in training? I'm proud of our men that serve our country. The women to. I don't know who this letter is going to or who is reading it. My teacher just told my class to write letters to Soldiers to let them know that you have our support Well you do and I will be with you all the way in your heart. I have a uncle over there his name is Gary Owens we don't know were he is stationed at he just left and didn't say much of anything. I worry about him and all of the other people that are fighting in the war. My friends Brandi Hunter & Alissa McDonald have relatives there to, but they are in the ~~marines~~ Mariens and might get drafted. I know they are worried to.

I'm pretty sure everyone is worried. IF I was standing right in front of Sadam Hussien. I would tell him kiss my rear!! I just can't stand him at all. And where was he during the war? I sure would like to know. Well I just wanted to...

Drop

a

few

lines and say (HI!!)

and everyone is worried and wants to win the war. So help all you can. And don't get hurt. Well I guess I'll talk to you later. IF you write me and send me your address, I'll write you back.

Stay Sweet,

Tiffany

Reynolds

P.S
My address is
on front and if
you want my phone #
Just for the heck of it, it is

Long Distance

its close to Boston!

Dear Tiffany,

Things are going fine here. Thanks for asking! We have ran into some Iraqi units, but so far things have been fairly quiet. I think you make a great point---there are many women in uniform too that are doing an excellent job---they don't seem to get enough recognition for their accomplishments. I appreciate your teacher for letting all of you write letters of support. You don't know how much all of us appreciate your letters. Thanks for being with us in heart. Your nice thoughts will be with me as we try to finish this war up over the next few weeks.

I bet your Uncle Gary Owens is fine. We all support and protect one another, so he is surrounded by friends that look out for him. Tell your friends Brandi and Alissa what I said about soldiers taking care of one another.

Well, if I happen to meet up with Saddam, I will pass on your message for him to, "Kiss your rear." You are not alone---not many people care for him. Maybe that is why he is so mean! Either way, don't worry. We WILL win this war and your family and friends will be home before you know it. I will try to write again. I have no way to get to a phone, so I can't call. Thanks for your spirited message! Like you close your letter....

Stay Sweet,

SSG. David Brown

Dear, Soilders

Hey, what are ya'll doing getting shot at. I hope ya'll ~~then~~ win the war. I want you to shot Saddam ~~Hussein~~ Hussein right in the forhead. I want you to shot him with a bazuka. Well I ~~am~~ am in Aubrey Texas its a little town but it will do. Maybe you can come and visit it some time. Its on the other side of Denton northeast side. I would like you to right back if you can. My number is ~~~~ Hill Rd. I think you are the best soilder ~~eventhough~~ eventhough I haven't seen you. I bet you want to now my name it is Bubba Bland. I would like for you to right back a soon as you can. Please don't forget about me what ever you do. Send me a picture of you please.

P.S. Don't forget
to write back
and send me
a picture!

Sincerlly,
Bubba
Bland

Dear Bubba,

Hey Bubba. Haven't been shot at yet---thank goodness! We will win the war. I doubt we will see Saddam Hussein, but somebody will eventually get to him and just maybe your wish will come true. Aubrey, Texas sounds nice. Who knows maybe one day I will get there. Thanks for thinking I'm the "best soldier," but I am just one of many and I am not too proud to admit, there are many who are better than I am. We have an incredible military. We all appreciate your support. Well, take care Bubba. Do well in school. Sorry, no camera here to take pictures at the moment. I'm funny looking anyway!

Thanks for writing!

SSG. David Brown

Dear Soldier,   1-19-91

I would like to express my hope for your success in Operation Desert Storm. I think it's very important that you help free Kuwait from Saddam Hussein. I believe that you guys will be able to do whatever is asked of you by President Bush. Saddam Hussein was wrong to take over Kuwait, and it's up to you to kick him out. In closing, I would like to say I think you guys will be able to free Kuwait.

Sincerly,

Jason Blalock
Mrs. Hunt's 6th
Aubrey, Texas

Dear Jason,

Thanks for your hopes of success. There is no doubt that we will succeed. In fact, I predict a quick victory. I also think it is important that we free Kuwait. The people there are innocent and do not deserve what Iraq has done to them. We will definitely do whatever President Bush asks of us. Kuwait will be free soon! Do well in school.

Your Friend in Iraq,

SSG. David Brown

Dear soldier,

Hi, I am at school right now writing you and I'm sort of confused about it all, but I am keeping you and all the other soldiers over there in prayer. It must be pretty scary over there. Two of my uncles are over there, one is in the airforce and the other is in the navy. Last night when my mom and my aunt were talking on the phone they said that should take the A-10's & and my other other uncles troop to Austraila "Just In Case" but I knew they were joking so they wouldn't be so scared.

Are you fighting right now. Everyone in my school has an opinion Each teacher tells us what they think and then at lunch time all the kids are blabbing, but most of them don't even know what their talking about. Do you think the war will last long. I was also wondering if ya'll ate good food or is it more like our cafeteria food? I am 12 and my name is Abigail Elizabeth Fretwell, I live in Denton Tex., and my dad is in the armed forces, What is your name and how old are you?

We are all so proud of everyone over there vol-enteering to fight for our country I will not forget you in my prayers. If you ever have time please keep in touch. Good luck— and remember you can't win without the Lord, bye b

Sincerely,
Abigail

P.S. Abigail Fretwell, 2005 Emerson,

Dear Abigail,

Hey Abigail. Yes, things can become very confusing even for adults during stressful times. War is a terrible thing, yet, is sometimes necessary to make sure people around the world remain free. It can be a little scary at times, but when things get bad, I think about my family and all of you in America and then remember how happy I am that you are safe at home---that makes me content.

I bet your uncles are fine. If you speak with them, tell them David Brown says thanks for their service. No, I am not fighting right now. As a matter of fact, I am out in the middle of the desert writing you. It is very peaceful at the moment even though I hear some explosions and gun fire in the distance. From the viewpoint of the desert, the stars seem to be so close you can grab them. It's really beautiful here at night.

Everyone has an opinion that is for sure. Just listen to them, let it in one ear and just as quickly, out the other. I do think this war will be over quickly---maybe in a few months---I hope. The food here is not too good. I would compare it to your cafeteria food, but then MREs are horrible, but you would be surprised what a person might eat when hungry.

My name is David Brown, and I am twenty-six years old. I am a Staff Sergeant in the U.S. Army. We arrived here just before Christmas.

Thanks for being proud of us. I am proud of you and your friends for being nice enough to write. Thanks for your prayers. We will definitely win with the Lord at our side. Thanks for reminding me!!

Your Friend,

SSG. David Brown

Dear Soldier,   ~~See~~ sorry 1-17-91
          Hi, what's going on over there.
Nothing here in Texas.
          I hope ya'll win your war.
Everybody ~~appreciates~~ oops appreciates how ya'll
 are fighting for are country. We all
are praying for ya'll.
 I get the point for the war but
why does Saddam think he can
take over. Kuwait has oil and stuff but
if Saddam get's a hold of it, do
you think he will give some to us.
He probably wont.
          I'm going to write about
something different. That subject
made me sad.
          So ~~I~~ did ~~it~~ ya'll oops get to see Bob Hope
and the other people that traveled with
 him. I think that was pretty
neat. I bet ya'll enjoyed it. I would.
          I'm going to give you some
information on who I am
I have brown hair, brown eyes, and I'm
really tan. ~~But~~ I stand about 4ft 9½ in
I'm in Sixth Grade and go to Aubrey High/middle
 School. And I am 12 years old. And my
name is Brandi Danielle Hurder. And → next page.

no I don't herd cows! (ha ha ha)

Right now I'm in math watching T.V. about ya'll. (and Saudi Arabia). It's pretty neat. But the war won't be. Coach LaDuke (my math teacher) is talking about the war. He's really in to it.

Anyways my brother, Chad Gresham, is in Great Lake ILLINOIS. He's in the navy. They said he can go anytime now. My brother is only 18. Me, and my family prays everyday. We pray for everybody in Saudi, Arabia. To get back to my brother. He went back to boot camp, or whatever ya'll call it, for the second time.

Just remember, the Lord is always with you, and we always pray for you and everybody there. Tell everybody I said Hi. (even though they don't know me). Well, Stay in touch if you can and remember were by your side all the way. Whoever this goes to were still praying and don't let Saddam take over. please please.

Well I'll tell you more about me. I have 2 best friends and alot of friends. My best friends are Alissa Denea McDonald. and Tiffany Rshell Reynolds. There realy nice. I'll name yoo my friend (some). Stacie Rodges, you, and everybody there, Patsi Starr, and alot of other people like Trina Brockett, Abigail Fretwell, and abunch of other people.

Well try to stay in touch and try to write.

Well I'm going to go. If you write me I will write you back.

Tell me if your a boy or a girl. Okay.

Love
Branch Hunter.

Were behind you all the way!

Dear Brandi,

What's going on over here? Well, we are in the middle of the desert dealing with the heat and bugs! I am in Iraq right now and we will be moving further north soon. We will win the war—do not worry. Thanks to you and the others who are supporting us, we are highly motivated to win quickly and get home. Saddam is a greedy man, and I doubt he would share the oil with us, but we do buy a lot of our countries oil from OPEC which is made up of Middle Eastern countries like Iraq, Kuwait, and Saudi Arabia.

No, we were unable to see Bob Hope. As a matter of fact, most of us didn't even know he was here. We are deep in the desert and they wouldn't want to send Bob Hope into danger (I wouldn't want them to either). Mainly the soldiers in Saudi Arabia will be able to go to the show. I would have loved to see him though.

Thanks for sharing the information about yourself. Don't worry, I didn't think you were a cow herder because of your last name. I imagine some of the little boys do though---am I right? Boys are just knuckle-heads! It must be nice to be able to watch TV and see what is happening with the war. We don't have TV or radio way out here. One day when I get home, I hope to watch some of the footage.

If your brother Chad ends up getting orders to Iraq, tell him to just take a deep breath and know we are all here to support him. That is what we do---we help one another. I hope your brother does well while training.

Thanks for the reminder that God is with us. I will share your letter with the others and tell them you said, "Hi." Don't worry, Saddam will not take over anything. His days are coming to an end very soon!

Thanks for telling me about your friends. It sounds like you have many of them. I can see why, since you seem very nice. Oh yeah, you asked if I am a boy or girl. If you didn't already know, I am a boy.

You are awesome, Brandi!

SSG. David Brown

Dear, Soldier,

Hey! How are you? Me,
O.K. I guess. This war is
making me depressed! You are
very brave! I envy you alot!
At first when the war
started, I thought, why are we
fighting for oil. But now I
realize that we are also
fighting for respect. And to let
Sadam Hussien know he can't
get away with this! He is
crazy in my opinion! Very crazy!
I've watched the news
alot, and so far we are
doing good! Israel and Great
Britian are really helpful also!
I'm glad we have such good
people on our side. And I'm
glad we have people like
you that contribute to the
war! I am still depressed
though! I feel so sorry
for all of the families that
have loved ones over there. And
I feel sorry for the soldiers too!

They don't know what's going to happen! But I hope and pray that everyone is O.K. after the war. But I guess I'd better let you go!

Good luck,

Stacy Thomas

Aubrey, Tx.
11yrs. 6th grade

P.S. If you have time, Please write me back! I would REALLY like for you to!

Dear Stacy,

I'm doing fine. Thanks for asking. No reason to get depressed about something we have no control over. Just stay positive and this will be over before you know it. Many people think we are here because of oil, but it is much more than that. The primary goal is to help Kuwait since Saddam Hussein and Iraq invaded and took the country over. We are here to get them out. I wouldn't say we are here to gain respect, but we will gain some respect around the world once this is over. Saddam is definitely a little mixed up and something has to be done to get him under control. Yes, there are many countries here helping out to include England, France, Spain, Canada, Syria, and many, many others. Together we will finish this up quickly.

Please don't feel sorry for the soldiers. We are paid to do the job we signed up for. We will be fine. On the other hand, it is sad for all of the families who miss their sons and daughters. Please do not be depressed. This will be over soon. In the meantime, whenever you feel yourself feeling down, pick up a pen and write. Writing always helps me feel better. Thanks for your letter and your support! I can tell you are a special girl.

Your Friend,

David A. Brown

1-17-91

Dear Soldier,

We don't know who you all are, but we have lots of ~~churches~~ churches praying for all of you, so do your best. I, myself, think you are very brave and we hope the all of you are able to come home. Thank you for fighting for us and our country.

P.S. I live in Aubrey Texas, my address is

I go to Aubrey High & Middle School.

Sincerly,
Misty Cardwell

Dear Misty,

No, you don't know who I am, but I am happy you chose to write. I am so glad to hear so many people are praying for us. The more the better. I will definitely do my very best!! Thanks for all of your kind words. Make sure you do well in school. Thanks for writing.

SSG. David Brown

Jan. 17, 1991

Dear Soldier,

We and my Class appreciate what your doing for the United States of America. I hope wich ever one of you reads this, that you and your troop survive the war. I also hope your families are fine. I'm sorry you couldn't be here for Cristmas and New Year. Good Luck with the war, I hope we win.

Sincerly,
Alfred Razor
Aubrey Tx.
6th. grade.

Dear Alfred,

I thank you for your appreciation. All of us over here are so happy thanks to all of the letters from you and many others. Don't worry---we will survive and we will be home very soon. I don't think things will last too long. I know my family is fine. They are in New Jersey with family, so they are well taken care of. I did miss Christmas and New Years with my family, but we did our best to celebrate it here. It wasn't quite the same and not nearly as fun, but I'm not complaining. Thanks for wishing all of us good luck. We will win.

SSG. David Brown

Dear American Soldiers,
My ~~name~~ name is
Monica Gilliland. I live
in Aubrey, Tx. I'm 12 yrs. old,
I am in the 6th grade. I am
praying for all of you. Hopefully, we will win what ever
this is. I love all of you.
My Teacher (Mrs. Hunt) told
us that you all valuntiered
to go knowing that I might
be war. That takes a lot of
bravery. I'm sorry about you
friend that went down. If
your not to busy could you
write me my add. is Monica Gilliland
one of or all of

Aubrey, Tx
76227

We (the 6th grade class of Mrs. Hunt)
are watching the CNN. update.

Hope we win
Love
Monica
Gilliland

Hey Monica,

How are things going in Aubrey? It's just a bit warm and dusty here. Thanks for your prayers. Like I told your friend Alfred (At least, I assume he is your friend), we will win, it's just a matter of how quickly. Your teacher, Mrs. Hunt, is correct in that we all volunteered in a way. We signed up for the Army by our own choice and we all knew that war was a possibility. Keep watching the news and maybe you will see me one day---oh yeah, you don't know what I look like---well, keep watching anyway so you know what is going on. Thanks for the nice letter.

Sincerely,

SSG. David Brown

Dear Soilder,

    Hello. My name is Stacie Rodges. I live in Aubrey Texas. I'm in the 6th grade, I'm 12 years old, and I go to Aubrey High/middle school.
    Which force are you in? I've got a cousin that might have to go down to Saudi Arabia also. His name is Larry Scott Rodges. He is in the army. I hope this war ends very soon. Well, I better go. Hope ya'll all get to come home very, very soon. God bless you ☺

    Sincerly,

    Stacie Rodges

P.S. We all have been praying for ya'll. You must be so brave!

Dear Stacy,

Hey, how is school at Aubrey Middle going? I bet you are a good student. You definitely write well! Thanks for writing. I am in the Army going on eight years. If your cousin, Larry Rodgers has to go to Saudi Arabia, don't worry because we take care of each other. He will have many friends and he won't be alone. I think things will end pretty quickly and maybe he will not have to go after all. Thanks for your prayers and nice words. Do your best in school and take care of yourself.

Your Friend,

SSG. David Brown

Dear solider,

Hi!! How are you? I'm not so great. I am really scared about the war. I don't have any one over there that I know. All of my friends say that the war will only last about a week or two. But I keep telling them that it will last for a while. I appreciate all of the soilders over there fighting for the United States. I also appreciate you risking your lives for the United States. Well I really don't have anything else to say just that: May God bless you all

Your friend,
Kinda Griswold of
the 6th grade
Aubrey, Texas

Dear Kinda (Again),

I'm kinda' tired today—get it? I'm just trying to have some fun. I think your name is beautiful. No need to be scared although it is normal during times of war. The best thing you can do is talk to your parents about how scared you are and they will help. Things will be alright though---I promise. Your friends are probably right that the war will only last a couple of weeks. We may end up being here for a while, but Iraq doesn't stand a chance. Thanks for all of your appreciation. I hope God blesses you too.

Your Friend,

SSG. David Brown

1/16/91

Dear, Soilder
I hope drive the Iraqis out of
Kuwait so it would return to normal.
I hope you come home without a scratch.
Make this war real short. And do something
with Hussien so he won't do it again.
Sincerly, Lopez, Gavino

Dear Gavino,

I hope you are doing well. We will get the Iraqi Army out of Kuwait—that is a promise. It may take a while even after the war has ended for things to go back to normal, but they will. So far, not a scratch and I like your idea to keep it that way! I doubt I will get to see Saddam, but I did get a glance of Baghdad (the capitol) from a distance. I wish I could have visited and toured the city. Either way, Saddam will be dealt with. Thanks for taking the time to write.

SSG. David Brown

Dear Soldiers, Hey! Yall having fun trying to kill Hussein. I know yall will kill him I'm sure glad you guys volunteered to go up there. My name is Billy Breon and I would like if you ~~guys to~~ wrote me back; I think you guys are the bravest men I ~~ever~~ ever seen.

Your Friend
Billy Breon

P.S. (Could you Possibly send me a bullet that you used or that hasn't been used).

P.P.S. My Address is [redacted] 76227
Aubrey T.X,

Dear Billy,

We are having some fun over here, but we will not be seeing Saddam any time soon. He sent all of his military into the desert, but I am positive he will not be out here---he's too wimpy. I don't know if he will be killed, but he will be punished for what he has done. As for your other question, no I cannot send you a bullet or the brass from a bullet---we are prohibited from mailing things like that, but I would gladly send you one if I could and if your parents gave permission. Thanks for writing Billy!

SSG. David Brown

Jan. 12, 1991
11:30 am.

Dear Soldier,

Hi! My name is Trina Brockett. I hope you're all okay (oops!) over there in Saudi Arabia. I'm praying for yall and so are all my friends + family. Let me tell you a little about myself. I'm 11 years old, but by the time this letter gets to you I'll be 12. I have blonde-brown hair and green eyes. I have two sisters, a brother, a brother-in-law, and a neice. I hope you don't think this letter is stupid but I don't know what to write!

If you can, I would like you to write back to me at
Aubrey, Tx. 76227 USA.
My sister met someone in Saudi Arabia by doing this. He is on a ship. You might know him. His name is Jim Greene.
other side →

I'm in my reading class at Aubrey High/Middle School. I'm in the 6th grade. I hope you are okay if you're fighting. I know we will win this war because we have ~~Israel~~ on our side and God is for Israel. As long as we have ~~<crossed out>~~ Jesus in our hearts and have faith in ~~<crossed out>~~ him, we'll be okay. But we have to thank God for whatever happens even if it's bad. He always does it for a good reason. It says this in the Bible. Well, I know if you ~~<crossed out>~~ have ~~<crossed out>~~ faith in him, he loves you and will let you be okay. I've got to go ~~now~~ now. Bye!

Sincerely,

Trina

P.S. Good Luck!
+ write back soon!

Dear Trina,

Hi Trina. Yes, we are doing fine. I hope you're doing well also. Thanks for your prayers. Also, Happy Birthday---Twelve years old---wow! You will be in high school before you know it. I do not think your letter is stupid at all. In fact, I appreciate it more than you will know. Tell your sisters and brother I said, "Hello." I'm sorry I don't know your sister's friend who is in the Navy. I am in the desert and definitely no water here. Your advice is the best I've heard: "Have faith in [Jesus], we'll be okay." Thanks for writing Trina! Maybe I'll hear from you again.

Your Friend,

SSG. David Brown

Dear, soilder,

We are praying for ya all the time over hear now. When we went to war I was real scared because my dad or brother can be drafted. Even my Grend parents could get drafted and when they do I will be very scared because they could get killed. Thats if they get drafted. All of you soilders out there fighting in the war are very brave. If we loose we would know that we have some good soilders fighting for us. I have a uncle there, are is supposed to. His name is Steven Short that he did live in maryland. If your out we will miss you.

your supporter
Shan, Davidson

Aubrey tx,
Spring hill rd.

What's happening, Shan or Shaun (Not sure),

I was so excited to get your letter. I love to read and lately haven't received too much of anything. It's rare we get mail out here in the desert of Iraq as of lately. I doubt very much a draft will begin---in fact, I can nearly guarantee it. I expect things will be finished very soon. You can hold me to that. We will not lose, so again, do not worry! We've got this handled. I am sure your uncle, Steven is fine too. No worries. Just worry about doing well in school and being with family. We've got this over here handled! Thanks for your support, Shan (Shaun).

Take care!

SSG. David Brown

Dear American soldier

Hi. My name is Bobbi Sparks. I am 11 years old, I live in Aubrey Texas. My address is

Aubrey, Tx
76227

Well we're all praying for you guys. We hope you don't get hurt. I just wish they would have settled this peacefully. Well I have 2 go 4 know. Bye Bye

Love Always,
Bobbi Sparks

Hello Bobby,

I have a brother named Bobby and my dad was named Robert or "Bob." You must be a pretty good guy to have such a cool name! We all wish this could have been settled peacefully, but Saddam is a stubborn person. No worries though. We will get him out of Kuwait very soon. You take care! Thanks for writing.

SSG. David Brown

Patsi Starr
[redacted]
Aubrey, Tx. 76227
age 11 grade 6
Date Jan. 17, 1991

Dear Soldier,

Hello! My name is Patsi, as you know. I live in Aubrey, Texas. I go to Aubrey Middle School. I am 11 years old, and I'm in the 6th grade. I want to talk about the war. I hate talking about things like this! My brother my have to go over in Saudia, his name is Steve Courple. He just got out of the Navy. I am sorry that you are over there. You are taking a big chance. You are really brave!! I pray for all the people in Saudia. I want to thank you, and all the other men in Saudia for standing up for our country. It really makes me mad when people don't give a flip. Oh well, if it wasn't for all you guys the our country would be destoryed By Butthole Saddam. I hate that guy!! I wish some brave soldier would blow him to pieces. If we don't destroy that mean man then he just might destory the whole world. I wish we knew where he was hiding, so ya'll could blow him up. Well, how's the desert over in Saudia? I would really like to know who you are, and where you lived. Do you know Steve Cowrple? If you do tell him I said "Hello!" I think Steve is cute, please don't tell him that! Are you married? Do you have any kids? By the way,

what do you look like?
I have light brown hair, I
have blue eyes (they have
little streaks of yellow in
them). Everyone says my
eyes are pretty, but I
think there ugly. Well,
I bet your TIRED of
reading so I'll let you
go. Bye? Bye? I'll pray for
you, and all the other
men in Saudia. I love, and
care for you!!

PS If you have
time then write
me. I would
love to know
who you are!!
I love, and
care for you!!

Love always,

Patsi
Starr

Dear Patsi,

I hope you are doing well. I bet it is hot in Texas this time of year. We average about 110 to 115 degrees here. It took some getting used to and the sand and dust makes it much worse. War is never easy to talk about. There is normally not much good about it, but in this case, we are helping the Kuwaiti people which is great. Hopefully, we will have things wrapped up before your brother has to deploy. Tell him thanks for his service in the Navy for me please. Yes, Saddam is kind of a "Butthole," like you say, but he will pay for his treachery. No, I don't know Steve Courple, but if I am lucky enough to meet him, I will tell him you were asking about him. I'll also be sure to tell him that you think he is cute---that's what you asked me to do, right?

You wanted to know who I am, so here is just a few details: My name is David Brown, I am a Staff Sergeant in the United States Army; I am twenty-six years old and have two kids, a boy and a girl. We lived in Germany before I deployed here. My family is going back to the states until I return. You also asked me what I look like so I will try to describe myself: I look like Tom Cruise with the body of Arnold Schwarzenegger. No seriously, I look a lot like a soldier; that is the best way I can describe myself. Does that help? Sorry, I couldn't be more specific. You have some cool eyes that sound pretty with the yellow streaks through them. I bet the boys at school like you but stay away from them. They have cooties!! Gross. Thanks, Patsi. You closed your letter with "Love always" and although I know very little about you, I feel like you would be easy to love. Your parents must be super-proud!!

Write again,

SSG. David Brown

Dear Soldier,

    I think you are doing a brave thing. I just wanted to tell you that I like the things your doing for a country. I'm sure your wife is worrying about you. Don't let that stop you.

        Your friend,
        Jimmy Hodge Aubrey I. 6th grade

Dear Jimmy,

I hope you and your family are doing alright. Thanks for writing and showing your support for us. We are working hard to get those Iraqis out of Kuwait. I imagine my wife is worrying like you said, but she is with family and they are taking care of her. I appreciate you writing. Do well in school!! You have to represent for the boys.

Your Friend,

SSG. David Brown

Dear Sr. or Mam,

I am a anamirican girl living in Aubrey Tx. I know it must be hard over there being away from home. I have a cosin, Chrissy Farmer who has a cosin over there. Operation Desert Storm must be hard to be envolved in. When you signed up to be in the U.S. armed forces you probly did not expect to be put in such a hot + dry clamit.

If you have time please wright me: DeeAnn Mullen
Aubrey Tx. 76009

Good Luck,
DeeAnn
Mullen

Dear DeeAnn,

Nice to hear from you again---I received another letter from you not too long ago. Thanks for writing so much! It is definitely hot and dry over here. One of my old units, while at Fort Carson, Colorado, deployed to Fort Irwin, California twice for desert training. The environment of the Mojave Desert isn't a whole lot different than here. With that said, it is difficult to adjust to the extreme heat especially while we often have to wear Chemical ---Mopp ---equipment. The coat and pants are charcoal lined and extremely hot. I will be glad to get out of here. Just a bit more to accomplish and we will be heading home, I hope. Take care!

SSG. David Brown

Dear American Soldier,
    I hope this letter may cheer you up a bit. My name is Megan McIntire I live in Aubrey, Texas and I'm in the sixth grade. I hope things turn out right for you. Meanwhile in school we have watched alot of news shows. Just finding out about what is happening in Saudi Arabia is scary. All the American Fighter Pilots must be scared to death just starting their missions. Well, I hope and pray for you, who gets this, that you shall come back to the United States soon and safely.
                    Yours Truly,
                    Megan McIntire
                    age 11
                    Aubrey, Tx

Dear Megan.

First, your letter definitely cheered me up. You will never know how much all of us here appreciate you taking the time to write. It is another super-hot day here. I am so tired of this heat. I bet it's hot in Texas too. I see the fighter jets flying overhead quite often. They are definitely brave pilots and they are doing an incredible job. Without them I believe we would have many more casualties. Unfortunately, I'm not a pilot. My unit is in the desert of

Iraq. I sure appreciate you writing! I hope you can write again soon. Don't be scared. We will handle things here and you just worry about school and your family and friends. I promise things will be fine. Take care.

Your Friend,

SSG. David Brown

Dear American Soilders,

I hope you don't get hurt! I'm rooting as much as I can! Anyways, my name is Jessica Jacobs. In my opioion I think the ~~th~~ Sadan Hussian Should have back out because I'm sure that we'll ~~bet~~ beat him. Truthfully I think he's dume for even coming and taking over Kuwaitt. I wonder if he thought he'd get away with it. But if he's stupid he probably thought that. I know that were going to ~~wiw~~ win because everything that we have is better (that's what I think). I bet your one of the best soilders there or if you are the best. Also, thank you for being so brave and volunterring to go to war. I was hoping that we didn't have to go to war! But Hussian thinks he has a chance (when he really don't). I think that is ~~stuos~~ was a good start ~~t~~ and a bad start to start the fight. I hope that the fight doesn't last long and that he'll get tired and finally realize that he don't have a chance! Remember, I'm with you all, the way! Do good! Bye!

Love,
Jessica
Jacobs

Dear Jessica,

I will be fine---so don't worry about me being hurt. I do appreciate your concern. We will all be fine here as long as we have patriots like you rooting for us. I agree with you that "Saddam should have backed out," but he is a little whacky and stubborn. It's just a matter of time and Kuwait will be free, and Saddam will face the consequences of his actions.

Our equipment is definitely better than theirs. We should end this quickly because of our advanced technology, since we have air superiority, and since we have so many countries in the coalition backing us. Countries like England, Canada, France, Belgium, Germany, and even Sweden have soldiers here. Even Middle Eastern countries like Syria and Saudi Arabia have troops helping out. Thanks for saying I am brave, but I am just doing the job I signed up for. Every job has its challenges and they are not always fun. Anyway, I just like that we all seem to be coming together as a nation. Sometimes the worst of events has unexpected consequences. From the letters I am reading, our country seems to be strongly united; I just wish it could stay that way! Thanks for being with us, "all the way"! Please write as often as you can.

Take Care in the meantime,

SSG. David Brown

Dear Brave Person,

Hi, my name is Cristal Rice. I am a 12 year old girl from Aubrey, Texas. I don't have much to say besides you are really brave. We are proud to have such fine people such as your self on our side. All the kids in my class are watching news on the televison about whats going on. We are behind you all the way. Thank you for being so brave. All of us are proud. I hope you guys can get in there and get it over with. We love all of you.

Love,
Cristal Rice

Dear Cristal,

I understand why you don't have too much to say; after all, it's difficult to write to anyone when you do not know who is on the other end. You say you are, "proud to have such fine people...on our side." I am proud to have people like you and the many others who take the time to show their appreciation and that express their thanks. I thank you for being so sweet and for being so giving. Thanks for being with us, "all the way." With people like you backing us, we cannot possibly lose!! In many ways, your letters---everyone's kind thoughts are what is going to lead to a quick and resounding victory. You are all soldiers in your own way.

Thanks, Private Cristal!

SSG. Brown

Dear
soldeer,
Our class is
writting to you and everybody else because
we know that we're going to kick some
butt!!,!!! Wherever this letter is
going whether its Saudi Arabia or
what, we know that we've got a great
chance of winning if congress will let
us. I hope we show them who is boss!!!!
Even though I'm a girl it would be
great for me to fight for my country.
Whoever is brave enough to fight for
there country is strong enough to win.
When I went to church the other day
all we did was pray for soldiers in
war such as Shane Cardwell, Jeff Carter,
Ronnie Owens, Chad Bresham, Vince Taylor,
Clint Sockwell and Kevin Sockwell, Tom Jones,
Tim Black, and Tony Stewart, I live in Aubrey
TX. and I go to Aubrey Middle School. I am
in the 6th grade. I don't have any
uncles or cousins actully in war now but
I know that its gotta be hard. GOOD
LUCK IN WAR! I hope we win!!!!!

Sincerely,
Amanda Busby

Dear Amanda,

 We are definitely going to "Kick some butt." I love your enthusiasm. Your letter did go through Saudi Arabia, but eventually made its way to me out in the desert of Iraq. It was actually perfect timing. It's now around 0100 hours (1 AM) and I just got back from a long day of unpleasant things. I sat down to find your letter and some others waiting. I opened yours first. You have no idea how much your letter helped. I was very frustrated and anxious, but your words cheered me up and reminded me how many good people there are out there. With so much violence and unimaginable things going on around us, sometimes it's easy to forget the unlimited amount of goodness that often surrounds us. You are part of that and I thank you.

You state, "Even though I'm a girl, it would be great for me to fight for my country." When you get older and begin to ponder what career path you want to follow, the military is a definite possibility. I'm not trying to convince you to join the military, but there are many women in uniform proudly serving over here in the Persian Gulf and around the world. I would gladly serve side by side with any of them. With that said, let me provide some advice. Whatever career path you choose, make sure it is a job that you will enjoy. Don't take a job just for the money. Instead, choose a job that you will enjoy doing and the additional benefit will be getting paid to do it.

It sounds like your church has been doing a lot of praying. Are all of the names you mentioned family members of the congregation? Tell the people in your church, thanks for the prayers. Thanks for your wish of, "Good luck."

You don't know how much I appreciate you!

SSG. David Brown

Dear Soldier,

Hello. My name is Alissa McDonald. I'm in the 6th grade, and I'm 11 years old. I live in Aubrey, Texas. And I go to Aubrey High/Middle school. I'm supposed to be writing what I fell about the war, so lets get right to the point. The war, I think, in some-ways ~~are~~ is good. But in others bad. The good reason is that it makes everyone care for each other. At church to show our support we have a huge board with ~~every cousin~~ everyones cousins over seas. My best friends brother is over there. His name is Chad Gresham. My other Best friends uncles is over there, too. ~~His~~ Thier names are Gary Owens and Ronnie Owens. Both of my Best friends don't know where their stationed at. So its pretty scary. So at church we pray for all the names on the board. We also pray for the ones that we don't know. So we pray for you.

In Bad ways, some people don't give a flip flop on whats happening. And don't care for anything or anyone. They wouldn't care if they were over there. But I care very much for each and _everyone_ of you.

Just a reminder we are Praying for all of ya'll.

God Bless
Alissa McDonald
Aubrey, Texas
76227

P.S. I would love ta here from you. like ta see who you are.

Dear Alissa,

You make a very astute observation when you state that war, "makes everyone care for each other." I have learned that no matter how bad the situation or event, some sort of good is a natural byproduct. In other words, good always comes from bad. One good thing that has happened for me since this war started is that I have been able to meet (through writing) so many amazing people---you are one of them.

I think that is a really neat idea concerning the bulletin board and the pictures of family members serving in the Persian Gulf. I bet your best friend's family members are on the board too. Am I right? I would expect to see a picture of Chad, and both Gary and Ronnie Owens on the board. Thank everyone for all of their prayers. The more the better! Thanks for caring so much for all of us here. Your kind thoughts are inspirational and help us to complete our job. Thanks!

With admiration!

SSG. David Brown

Dear: American Fighter

I don't know you but it feels like every one that is standing behind yall is one big family. I think we will win this war if everyone sticks together. But if no one believed that you could do it you'll be in trouble. Every one believes though so we will win this war. Saddam is going to wish he never started this war after we get through with him. Keep fighting for good and especialy for our country. I wish I could be over there fighting because I believe in what yall are doing. I think that we are doing whats best for our country.

I hope you get home safe.

Love Your
American Friend

Robert
Bridgman

P.S. This is Saddam when we finnish with Iraq

Dear Robert,

Wow, what a lifelike and hopeful picture of Saddam! Nice. This war has united many of us and like you said, we seem to be, "one large family." What a great way to look at things. We are all supporting one another. It would be hard for us to go on over here if it wasn't for the support you express through your letters. In many ways, you and everyone who is writing are just as responsible for our success here in Iraq as we are. Your inspirational words and prayers keep us motivated and inspire us to try harder.

I think you are right about Saddam wishing he never started this war. Who knows what was going through his head? I appreciate your desire to be over here and fight, but you handle things on that end. Do well in school, support your family, and we will take care of Saddam. Like you said, we are all one big family, and we have to take care of one another. Your job is just as important as mine! Again, thanks for the artwork and the very nice letter.

SSG. Brown

Dear Fighter,

Hello. I just wrote fighter because I didn't know who this was going to. Whoever it maybe I would like to tell you THANKS for protecting our country. I don't really know what to say. I (just) wish we could just shot ~~the~~ Saddam Hussein but he has to many people behinde him. Anyway be carefull and keep up the good work.

Love
Trina Micell
Aubrey Jr. High/High schoo
6th grade

Thanks

Hey Trina!

I hope you are doing well. Thanks for writing. That's fine if you call me fighter. It's is hard to write to a person when you don't know who will be on the other end to receive it. Don't you worry, we will take care of Saddam's army and he will eventually face the consequences of his actions. Thanks for writing---write again if you get the chance.

Sincerely,

SSG. David Brown

Dear Soldier,

Hey dude! I'm Craig Arrington and I live in a little town called Aubrey in Texas. I really hope yall kill Sadam Hussein. We all are praying for yall. I hope yall don't have to fight "just the air force." But if you have to fight remember we're praying for you. So when you do fight don't freak out just fight and we'll win. Yall are really brave & we all respect you all and what your doing.

Sincerely
Craig Arrington

P.S. Blow em away.

If you can write back:
Rt 1 Box 171 A Aubrey Tx
PLEASE

Hello Craig!

Cowa-Bunga, dude! I'm sorry, that was kind of nerd-like. I just immediately thought of the Ninja Turtles when you opened with "Hey dude!" Our Air Force conducted many strafing runs and bombed a number of sites, but the ground troops are doing most of the job now with the Air Forces support. I promise, I almost freaked out a few times, but we supported one another and we made it through the chaos. Thanks for writing and thanks for your support!

SSG. David Brown

Tiffany Reynolds

Aubrey TX 76227

Dear, Solider,

      Hello! My name is Tiffany I am 11 yrs old and I am in the 6th grade. I'm real sad about the war, But I'm pretty sure we will win. We have better resoreses than Sadam has. There are lots of questions that I want to ask about the war like; Were was Sadam during the war I didn't see him out making any Commands? And our president was out making speeches, telling people what to do, and how to be safe. No one will answer questions like this for me. And I don't see why there's nothing wrong with it. They are just simple questions wich teaches children like me about it. Well I only have one relative at the war, but I don't know where he is stationed his name is Joe Owens. My friends Alissa McDonald and Brandi Hurder have relatives there to. Brandi's brother is in the Marions and might be drafted. Everyone at churchs are prayin for the people there. If you watch t.v you could probably tell. Well I gotta go.

            Love, Tiffany

Dear Tiffany,

I received another of your letters, maybe a third one, over the last couple of weeks. Thanks for writing so much! Don't be sad about the war. It is a natural reaction to bad things, but just think about all of the good that will come from this conflict. First, the Kuwaiti people will be free and not have to worry about being hurt by the Iraqi occupiers. Second, the war is helping to unite the world as well as our country. Our country may also become allies with some countries that at any other time might have been impossible. I know the people of the United States are coming together and forgetting the trivial differences, so there are many things to celebrate and make you---all of us—happy in this very dark time. Focus on the good is the best advice I can give.

Our resources are definitely better than Saddam's and we also have a huge coalition of countries backing us. Countries from around the world have troops here just as ready to fight as we are. You make a good point when you ask, "Where was Saddam during the war?" You will not see Saddam on the battlefield. He sent his army and will probably abandon them once we defeat them. He is worried about himself. Most tyrants are not normally worried about others. I love your inquisitive side. I know the president was trying to ease the people's worries. We can't have him on the battlefield since that would put the leader of our country in danger and he is needed there. He has Generals to lead the war in the Persian Gulf. If you have any other questions, just send them to me and I will try to answer them for you. I know it is sometimes frustrating as a child when adults forget or sometimes overlook the very important questions children have.

I hope your family member, Joe Owens is doing well. I bet he is fine. I received letters from Alissa and one from Brandi and they mentioned that they had family involved in Desert Storm. You mention Brandi's brother might be drafted. Just a minor correction; he would be deployed not drafted.

Thanks for your support and for the awesome questions, Tiffany!

Peace to you too!

SSG. David Brown

Dear Solister,   Jan. 17, 1990

          I know you don't know me — I'm in
the 6th grade, I'm 11 years-old. I know you
don't care what a little kid think. Stuffe about the
war as been on every channels today and last
night and on all the raido stations. In frist
period we listen to the raido stations and drew
maps of the Middle East. In 3 period we watch
CNN on T.V. and were doing the same in
4 period and writing these letters. I bet it hot
there! I wish you could have supnd Christmas
and Thankgiving with your flaimy. Do you
have a wife in American? My name is Randi
Michelle Bland, but I like to be called Michelle.
My farther name is Randy Ray Bland.
He was in the Army and if they have to
do the draft hes going to have to the Middle
East and I don't want him to go. He a plice
officer now. If you have time write me please.

          A nice preson,
     (Randi) Michelle Bland

Hey Randi (Michelle),

You begin your letter with the statement, "I know you don't care what a little kid think(s)," but I think your opinions and thoughts are very important. I imagine every channel is full of news on the war, the support, the protests, and what is happening here in the Persian Gulf. I imagine it can become kind of annoying after a while since you also are watching the news about the war in school too. It's good that you are aware of what is going on around the world.

It is very hot here, but from what I understand, it is very hot there in Texas too. Things could always be worse. Yes, I wish I were with my family for Christmas, but many nice people like you sent care packages with some snacks and things we needed. We celebrated the best way we could. The people around me are my family too, so I wasn't alone. I hope you had a great Christmas.

Yes, I am married. My wife's name is Susan and we have two children, David and Ashleigh. I don't think your dad has to worry about being drafted. I doubt the draft will be put in place since this conflict will be over very soon, so try not to worry. Tell your dad thanks for his service for me. Take care of yourself and thanks for writing.

With admiration,

SSG. David Brown

Dear Soldier,

Hi my name is Tonya Redfearn and I'm 11 years old. I go to Aubrey Middle School. It's hard for me not to cry. Because I'm very scared about the war. You must be very brave to volentere to fight for our country. I hope we win the war. I am praying for all of you soldiers. When I found out about the war I got worried. But I thought to my self if we did not have oil [sorry] our cars would not run or machines either. My Mom was worried to. At school we are watching the news alot. I think it is very interesting

over

~~Saddam Hussein~~

Err!!!

Saddam Hussein makes me very mad. Every time I think of him I get very angry. I think he is a geek. He just makes me sick. Well I'm running out of words to say. So I've got to go.

Tonya Redfearn

P.S. If you have time write back Because I would really like to hear from you.

Tonya Redfearn
Aubrey, Texas
76227

Also I care for you and I no you and all of the other soldiers can win the war

Dear Tonya,

First, please do not be scared. I know it is natural to be scared, but have confidence that we are handling things here. You are not in danger---your parents will take care of you there and we will make sure you are safe on this end here in the Persian Gulf. So, while tears can be healthy, there is no need to cry---you are safe!

We will win the war and I don't think it will take too long. We have better equipment, we are better trained, and we have air superiority (Fighter jets).

Many people think that this war is all about oil, but it is much more than that. The coalition of many countries would never have supported a war if it were only about oil. First, we wouldn't be here if Iraq wouldn't have invaded Kuwait. Our primary mission is to free the people of Kuwait. Second, yes the war was partially about oil, but not like so many people think. Kuwait is part of OPEC and they supply a lot of oil to our country. They are an ally and we had to help them out on a humanitarian basis as well as make sure that their oil was accessible. I am no politician, but I do not believe that this war started because we wanted to steal another countries oil or claim the oil wells as ours. This is a war driven by humanitarian purposes.

You are not the only one mad at Saddam. People around the world are angry with him. I don't know if he is a "geek," but then again, I will take your word for it. Thanks for caring for me. I care for you also and hope I helped to ease your anxiety—don't worry, we will handle Saddam. You just worry about doing well in school and being with your family.

Sincerely,

SSG. David Brown

January 21, 1991

Dear Soldier,

Hi! My name is Delinda Musgrove. I'm not much of a writer, I just wanted you to know that I'm all for you guys! In history we are learning about the Middle East. In science we drew a map of the Middle East. In all of the other classes we watch the news. This was all the day after the war began.

I'm in 6th grade and I'm 11 years old. My birthday is in April.

I hope this war is over soon!

Do you drop bombs on Iraq or are you a land person?

Well I'm watching the news at school. This war is pretty scarey! I hope this war does not last long! It probaley will though!

Everybody wants you and everybody to come home as soon as possible.

I hope Saddam Husien doesn't bomb Isreal any more. He will I bet! But we can stop him! I know we can!

Keep Well!

I hope you come hope soon!
Delinda Musgrove

P.S. — If possible please write back! Here is my address!
Delinda Musgrove
Aubrey, Texas 76227

Hey Dee Dee,

I responded to another one of your letters not long ago. Nice to hear from you again! I think it is cool that you are able to watch the news while in school. It's important to stay up-to-date on current events.

No, I am not in the Air Force, so I do not drop bombs on people although I wouldn't mind doing that! I am in the desert in Iraq. Our job is to meet up with the Iraqi Army and destroy them as they exit Kuwait. So, I guess you can say we are, "Land people."

Yes, war can be very scary, but remember that you are safe in America. Your mom and dad will keep you safe and we here in Iraq will take care of things here---no worries. I don't think the war will last for too long. We have already made great progress. I want to come home as soon as possible too, but I want to make sure that Iraq and Saddam are no longer a threat before we leave, otherwise, we are wasting a lot of time. Well, thanks for sharing your thoughts. Take care at home and when you begin to feel scared, just think about all of the good things around you: Family, friends, your church, the peace you enjoy, and I hope those thoughts ease your fear. I hope to hear from you again.

Your Friend,

SSG. David Brown

Tiffany Reynolds

Aubrey Tx 76227
age 11 grade 6
Date Jan. 17. 1991

Dear Solider,

Hello! My name is Tiffany as you probably know. I am 11 yrs old. I think this war is good in some ways and bad in others. In a good way it teachs people resonsibility and it bringgs people to care more for others. In a bad way there are people who don't give a flip about anything. As for me I think that we should support you and other soliders and stand by ya'll with great honer. Thats the least we could do, think about it you and others are fighting for our lives. Every Wensday night me and my friends go to church and pray that people at Saudia Rabia are going to be safe and that the lord is with them and you all the way. My grandmother said that she thought the war wouldn't last very long. And that we would win. I wish that is the way it would be, but I think it is going to last for a little while longer. I have a relitive up there his name is Gary Owens we don't know where he is stationed at. All he did was just leave about 2 days ago. And he didn't call we don't even know if he is alright. I hope he is, cause I really care for him a whole lot, I care for everybody there. And I just want everyone to be very careful and watch what your doing. Everytime I hardly even think about the war and people getting killed. I want to brust out crying. I do sometimes. I just want to crawl into a hole and when it's all over have someone come get me and tell me everything is alright, but I know I can't do that I guess I am just going to have to put up with it. And put up with everything around me. I know everone thinks the same about this. If your one that is fighting or is going to. I will pray for you and think about you always.

Good luck.

Tiffany
Reynolds

P.S
If you ever have time could you write me back. To see who you are? I would love to hear from you.

Hey Tiffany. It's so nice to hear from you again. I included this letter because, while it states mainly the same things as the other two letters you sent, your hand writing is so perfect. I thought it would be a shame to leave it out. You don't know how honored I am to get another letter from you. You mention that people "should support...and stand by y'all with great honor." Likewise, I think that us soldiers should support and hold you in great honor. Without your inspirational messages and you taking the time to write, we would be alone out here and not know how much support we really have. In many ways, you are helping us to win this war. Thank you and don't worry, we are all being very careful.

Instead of thinking about people dying, think about all of the lives being saved, and you will feel better. I can tell you know that things will be alright, so do not "crawl into a hole." Be there for your family and friends. I can tell you are a very caring person, but I also sense a very strong young woman inside. I will pray for you too.

Your Friend, SSG. David Brown

February 21, 1991

Dear David:

I just wanted to write you a letter to let you know that I am a Mother of a child from Whittier Christian Junior High School who recently wrote you a letter. Your response to his letter arrived yesterday at his school and he brought it home and shared it with us. I just wanted to thank you myself for such a nice and warm response. We all have enjoyed hearing from you.

We pray for all of you every day. God is the only one who has control of this situation we are in. We just hope this is all over soon and you are all back home with your families.

To show our support to all of our troops, we wear yellow ribbons with small American flags and place yellow ribbons on everything that we can. We care so much about all of you and pray for your safety and protection every day.

I am a parent just as you are. I know you must miss your family so much and are anxious to get back home.

I work for Rockwell International in Downey, California as a Secretary. Just to let you know that Rockwell very much supports all of you too.

I enjoyed reading your letter and reading about what you do there in Saudia Arabia. It sounds very interesting. I know that the kids sure enjoyed hearing from you. You are all very loved and missed here in the states and we are looking forward to this war being over. We intensely listen to the news everyday and keep abreast of what is going on.

David, I will keep you in my prayers and hope that you are back home very soon. I wish you well and I ask you to keep praying too. God does answer prayer.

Your friend,

Karen

Karen Collins

Norwalk, CA 90650

Dear Karen,

I am thrilled that your son and family were able to share my reply. Of course, all these years later, I do not remember what I wrote, but I am sure it was heart-felt. In fact, I do not know if I ever responded to this letter once I received it. I apologize if I didn't. I just wanted you and your family to know how important your response was to me. I didn't get many responses to my letters. Yours sticks out in my mind even all of these years later. Thanks for your prayers back then. If you happen to come upon this publication, please do not hesitate to contact me. I would love to know how you are doing all these years later!

Your Friend,

SSG. David Brown

Dear Mrs. Hunt,

I wanted to thank you from the bottom of my heart for letting your students write to us soldiers. Their letters were inspirational and a lot of fun to read. I placed a copy of your business card below hoping one day you will locate this book and get my message. You must be or must have been an awesome teacher. The kids seem to love you. Thanks again!

SSG. David Brown

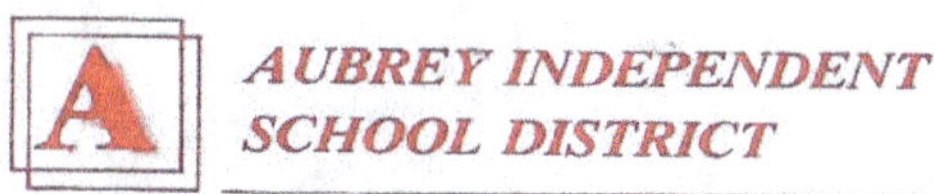

CAROLE HUNT
Professional Educator

From a student who attended Ferndale Baptist School in North Charleston, North Carolina

Dear Whitney,

All of my friends enjoyed your letter and creative art. Yes, we are fine, just a little hot and tired, but all is well. I bet all the boys in your class think you are pretty. Thanks for the picture. By now you have graduated from school. I hope you are happy and very successful.

I also received letters from the **Mojave Elementary School located in Mojave, California**, but all I found was the empty envelope. I am sure that I thoroughly enjoyed every one of the letters from each student. Thank you!

CHAPTER 2

BUSINESSES

While many schools decided to write and send their thoughts and hopes, a number of businesses and colleges thankfully took the time to send their best wishes and kind words. The letters that follow are some of those that I received and shared with many of my colleagues. We all are extremely thankful for you reaching out and for your support. I only have a couple of letters from these businesses, but I remember many letters from others that I no longer have. I want to take the time to thank each and every company, corporation, and organization for the support you provided. I can attest to the powerfully motivating impact that each and every well-wish letter meant to soldiers throughout the Persian Gulf War zone. Thank you!

RUTGERS
COOPERATIVE
EXTENSION
of Atlantic County

1200 West Harding Highway
Mays Landing, NJ 08330

NEW JERSEY AGRICULTURAL EXPERIMENT STATION   609/625-0056

Dear Friend,

We would like you to know that you are always in our thoughts and prayers. And **CONGRATULATIONS ON A JOB WELL DONE!!** We are employees of the Rutgers Cooperative Extension in Atlantic County. We are an educational branch of Rutgers University. Our purpose is to serve the residents of Atlantic County in the areas of agriculture, home economics and the 4-H youth development programs.

We want you to know we are well informed through the radio and TV as to what is happening where you are stationed. There are some of us who have family members and friends serving in the military. We are proud of ALL of our SONS, DAUGHTERS, HUSBANDS, WIVES, BROTHERS, SISTERS, FATHERS, MOTHERS and FRIENDS who serve our Country and defend it for ALL of us who remain behind in the USA. We want you to know that we fly our American flag, day and night, attach yellow ribbons on our homes and places of business and wear red, white and blue and yellow ribbons on our shirts and blouses as a symbol of our support for YOU. We are told on TV that the flag industry can hardly keep up with the demand of flags that American citizens are purchasing. I guess Betsy Ross would be proud to know that what she has created, many, many years ago, has become one of our traditional symbols of our American heritage.

Our hopes, dreams and prayers are with every serviceman and woman on foreign/home soil, that you return home to all of us, safe and very soon!

You are where you are to serve and protect us as American citizens; we would like the opportunity and privilege to serve you, if we can. If you need or want anything, please let us know.

GOD PROTECT YOU!

Your Friends,

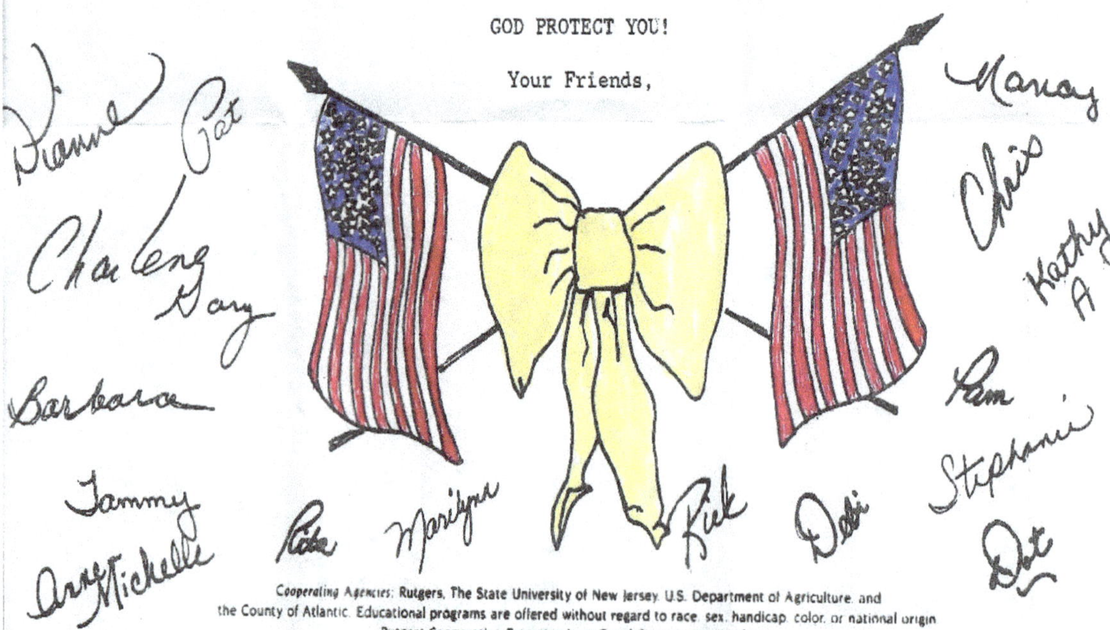

Dear Employees of the Rutgers Cooperative Extension,

Thanks for writing and for all of your well wishes. It was nice to hear how local communities are supporting the troops by proudly flying the American flag, displaying yellow ribbons, and wearing red, white, and blue clothing. Wouldn't it be nice if our country could remain this united even in times of peace? It's sad that it often takes a catastrophic event to bring the people together. Thank you for all of your prayers! We'll be back soon and I hope all of your family members serving in the Gulf are well. Thanks again for writing.

SSG. David Brown

THOMAS M. STARK, D.D.S., M.S.D.
PRACTICE LIMITED TO ORTHODONTICS

AMES, IOWA 50010

19 Mar 91

GREETINGS FROM IOWA !!!!

A group of us from our office here in Ames, Iowa decided we'd like to show our appreciation (although in a small way!) by getting together a "goodie box". Hope you'll find all this useful!

If you, or anyone else there would like to correspond, please let us know - we'd be glad to write!

We want you all to know how **PROUD** we are of you and our prayers are with you.

Wishing you a safe and speedy return!

Cindy Kane
Carla Hatten
Barb Carlson
Andrea Kuehl
Tom Stark
Nan Allen
Susan Carter
Willa Callahan
Jennifer Downs

Dear Cindy, Carla, Andrea, Tom, Barb, Nan, Susan, William, & Jennifer,

I am positive the things you sent were well received and very much appreciated. Thanks for taking the time from your busy schedules to put the care package together. I thank all of you from the bottom of my heart. Thanks for your prayers and for supporting us. We all hope to have the "Safe and speedy" return that you wish for us. Thanks again for writing!

Sincerely,

SSG. David Brown

This letter arrived from a person working at Roger Williams General Hospital (Pathology and Laboratory Medicine Dept.) located in Providence, Rhode Island.

February 1, 1991

Greetings,

I'm writing to you today to let you and all the military personel know that the U.S. public is behind you 100%. We are very proud of the military success so far. So keep up the good work and hopefully we'll be seeing you all back here real soon.

I hope you enjoy this comic. Be sure to pass it on. I can't write much more because I'm at work right now. However, before I go, I'll tell you a little about myself. I'm 22 years old and just graduated from college in Massachusetts. I work in the chemistry laboratory in a hosipital in Providence, RI. I spend most nights watching CNN until 3 am trying to find out what it's like over there and what is going on. The coverage isn't too bad at all but very repetitive. I hope you're all healthy & safe. You'll be hearing from me soon.

God Bless

David Gremza

N. Scituate RI 02857
USA

Write back if you have time

P.S. Kick some Iraqi Ass!!
If you need anything, let me know.
USA #1

Dear Mr. Gremza,

Thanks for letting us know that the public is behind us. We occasionally get letters that mention the protests which is disappointing. The comics were a well needed diversion. I am so glad you shared them with all of us. They were passed around to nearly the entire unit. I imagine working in a Chemistry Laboratory is very interesting. I appreciate your hope for all of us to remain healthy and safe. By the way, as I am sure you have known, we did "Kick some Iraqi ass" like you requested. You are right---USA #1. Take care.

Your Friend,

SSG. David Brown

CHAPTER 3

DISTANT FAMILY, FRIENDS AND LOST LETTERS

It was very early morning, near 0200 hours after the hostilities wound down for the evening. My fatigues were soaked from collar to ankle, my mind still processing the extraordinary images that demanded interpretation and awaited a place to inhabit until fully internalized. Normally, the mind easily compartmentalizes everyday experiences and places them in our subconscious in an orderly manner, but the previous day's events, the events witnessed that evening, disrupted normal operations. A whole new category had to be established to coral the unimaginable calamity of that day and the events of the days and weeks that followed.

The immense pressure and level of stress that comes with war at times becomes overwhelming, especially when sleep deprived. After functioning in such a hyper-vigilant state for an extended period, the things we sometimes take for granted assume a heightened presence. Even in the midst of the battle, care packages served to ease tensions and provide, if only for a moment, a well needed distraction from extremely taxing events. Normally, a couple of times a week, mail would be delivered no matter where we were in the desert. The system was more reliable than the U.S. Postal System in the states although the packages were sometimes mutilated or the perishables inside, molded and past their freshness date. During mail call , most individuals would go immediately to the larger packages labeled to "Any Service Member," since they were normally loaded with goodies and the essentials like shave cream, toothpaste, soap, and other necessities. For me, while others darted for the packages, I went directly to the letters. The letters from schools, churches, anonymous individuals, and of course, family and friends, would whisk me away from the immediate worries and temporarily deliver a great level of joy. The people who selflessly took the time to write these letters and send care packages often provided the little extra push each soldier needed to press on and get the job done.

The letters that follow are from friends and family that I honestly did not know I had or that I may have met once or twice, but up until the time that Desert Storm occurred, our lives never crossed again. Many knew my wife and others simply wrote because other family members compelled them to do so. Whatever the case, I was excited to receive your words of support and inspiration.

Many of my friends and fellow soldiers also read your letters, especially when we were deeply embedded in Iraq and mail rarely arrived. I believe that each person I shared your letters with felt as if they were part of the family and at a minimum, took something meaningful from your correspondence. On many occasions my squad members and colleagues shared letters from their families with me and I admit the words of strangers, the words of somebody else's family oftentimes brought me great happiness and a level of contentment that was desperately needed.

Without the support of families in particular, our jobs would have been so much more difficult. The loving words of family make a powerful impact that at times whisks a person away in memories, the memories that bring forth so much joy, that at times cause the worries and anxiety of what was going on around us, to seem to dissipate momentarily. Later, these thoughts provided a boost of energy, much like adrenaline, and became a catalyst that helped us to drive on through the adversity.

January 18, 1991

Dear Dave,

I am not sure you will remember us but I am Bob Maholland's cousins. We last saw Susan + the children at Nancy and Bill's house in Trenton. Susan sent us your address in the Christmas card.

Even though we have not written earlier, you have been in our prayers both at home and at Church.

Our family has been glued to the TV for the past two days. We read with interest the news in the paper.

I am very concerned about you and your fellow troops. I had always hoped that Vietnam would be our last involvement in conflict.

Please recognize that everyone I have contact with speaks highly of the commitment of our troops. Yellow ribbons and American flags seem to be almost everywhere!

We will continue to pray (over)

for your safety and a speedy end to this war.

Sincerely
Diana

Hi. Haven't seen you since the wedding many moons ago. I hope you are safe. The news today (1-18-91) is reporting good results with the air strikes, and we can only hope things continue to go well so Mr. Hussein gets kicked out soon.

The country is behind your efforts (and the rest of your buddies, since stability in the Mideast is so important to our oil supply. (Perhaps, soon, we may be able to be less dependent on it). The A.C. Nielsen company (the T.V. rating people) said President Bush's speech on T.V. after the bombing raids started was watched by over 70% of the country, more than the percentage of people who watched the Kennedy assasination (and burial) weekend.

If you get a few minutes to write, let us know your situation. I spent about 8 months in a 10 man tent in VietNam back in 1964/65. Not bad, except during a couple of heavy rains and a hurricane.

Please take care, and keep your head on straight.

Regards,
"Cousin Charlie".

Dear Diana & Cousin Charlie,

It's been so long that I am having trouble picturing either of you, but I wanted both of you to know I was moved by your message. I think my father in law, Bob Maholland, is a great man who served in the police for decades. I always looked up to him, so any friend/family of his is a friend of mine. I am glad you sent the Christmas card. Thanks for keeping me in your prayers and being concerned about the troops, but we are alright. It's nice to know that the country is supporting us in so many ways. Charlie, I like your idea of not being so dependent on the Middle Eastern countries for oil. Energy independence would be empowering for our nation. It is hard to believe that over 70% of the country watched president Bush's address to the nation following the bombing raids. Our country is weakened by the bickering and divisive efforts of so many hate groups and agencies. I wish people would join together in admonishing the hateful forces in our country. We would all be so much better for our efforts. We are strong together and weaker when segregated. Thanks for your service in Vietnam in 1964-65. You are a true hero. Thanks for writing. I hope to meet up with both of you again once I get home. Take care!

SSG. David Brown

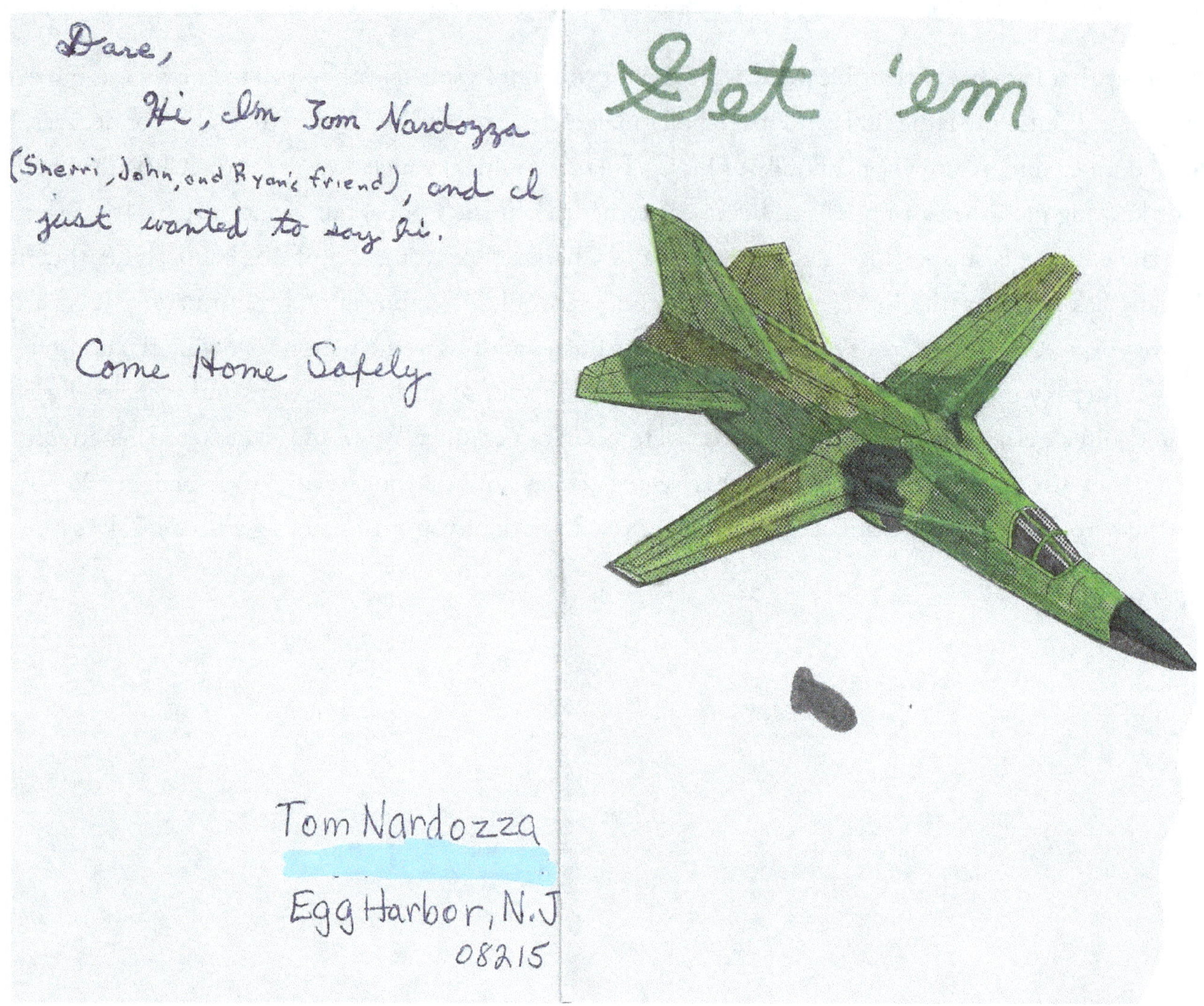

Dear Tom,

I hope you are doing well. I just received a letter from Sherry and John not long ago. Thanks for sending the card and your thoughts. I was wondering, did you draw that bomb under the plane or was the card made that way? I always wondered. I hope you are doing well. Hope to be home safely very soon.

SSG. David Brown

January 25, 1991

Dear Dave,

    Even though we have met only a couple of times, we wanted you to know that we are concerned about you and hope that everything is well with you considering the situation. We pray for you and all the men and women that are over there and that you will all come home soon.
    We received a very nice Christmas card and letter from Sue explaining that you had left for the Persian Gulf. We did not receive it until after you had already gotten there.
    You would be very proud and happy to see the support that everyone here is giving all of you. Flags are flying, yellow ribbons everywhere and I understand that on Sunday, January 27 at 4:00pm sirens, horns, etc. will blow all over the USA in support of everyone involved in this war.
    Everyone is glued to their TV or radio to keep up with any news on what progress is being made to rid this madman from power. We feel that the United States and their allies are doing a good job and hope that this war ends soon and all of you will be back with your loved ones again.
    Dave, we plan to write Sue again soon and see if there is anything we can send you.
    Take care and we send our love to you.

Love,

Aunt Nancy and Uncle Bill

Hello Aunt Nancy & Uncle Bill,

It was great to hear from you. Prayers are always welcome, but don't worry, we will be fine. We all hope to be home soon. I have heard about the unwavering support from Americans around the country. On the other hand, I have also heard about large protests, but hope they will dwindle as time progresses and as we get closer to a victory. Another family from New Jersey also mentioned the January 27th event where horns and sirens would be sounding off at 4:00. I would have loved to have been there. No T.V. or radio for us here on the front lines. We do occasionally get a news clipping or a newspaper via mail which is always nice but normally are weeks old. I feel so out of touch with what is going on around the world. Thanks for keeping in touch with Susan and the kids. Write again if you can.

Love,

Dave

Jan 4th

Hello Dave,

Just a few lines to let you know we're thinking about you. We pray this ordeal will be over quickly & without many (or any) casualties. Please take care & know we're behind you. We'll help out Sue & the children when they need us too.

Sincerly,
Jim, Donna &
Brandon Bennett

Dear Bennett Family,

Nice to hear from you. Thanks for helping Susan and the kids. It's a relief to know that we have you and others to look out for our families while we are away. We all hope there will be a quick conclusion to the hostilities and of course, that there will be no or very few casualties. Stay in touch.

Love,

Dave

-1-   1-19-91

Hi David

You don't know me but I'm a neighbor of your mothers. We were talking today and I didn't realize she had a son in Saudi Arabia. My cousin is there also - Capt. Vince Leone. Its so hard for us to imagine what you guys are going thru. We watch minute by minute on T.V. The people of this country are so fortunate to have such an awesome military. I for one am so proud of all of you. There are a few protestors over here but they represent such a small percentage of America. Always a few bad apples. Everywhere we go - American flags are flying and orange ribbons are all over

-2-   1-19-91

the place. You guys are all our heroes and if old "whats his name" over there was smart he'd realize who he was up against and beg you all to stop! Takes some people a while to learn huh? I wish there was more we could do here besides give blood + pray. You are on our minds every minute of every day. I have a son who is almost 11 yrs old. The Army, Airforce, Navy Marines - they are all so awesome to him - he's young - he's a dreamer - he's seen top gun 20 times - he's far from reality! But I look at him and wonder how hard it must be to have a son at war, and yet how proud a mother must feel. After

-3-   1-19-91

Talking to your mother and seeing a great wealth of pride in her I just want you know how proud she is - its written all over her face. I hope David when you come home I have the privilege to meet you! I'll look forward to that! Thanks for being so brave and doing such an excellent job for all of us! Will write again soon.

You're all our heroes - may God bring you home soon!

Mike + Leslie Meills

Dear Mike and Leslie Meihls,

Thanks for writing when you don't even know me. I agree with you when you state our "Military is Awesome," and that we are a lucky country. I hope you have heard from your cousin, Captain Vince Leone, and that he is doing well. The one universal message sent by so many writers is that the country is behind us and at the same time, there are some protests going on. War is a very difficult thing to support when it results in killing and suffering, but at times, extreme measures have to be taken to insure future freedoms and prosperity. I'm glad my mom has nice friends like you. Thanks for being there for her. I do not believe we ever had the pleasure of meeting, but perhaps one day in the future. I appreciate your kind words. Take care!

SSG. David Brown

Mixed amongst the letters I managed to hang onto, I located a set of envelopes with addresses, but no letters inside. At the time, I am sure these envelopes contained letters, but between all of the movements and the hostilities, I managed to lose them. While I regret that I do not have letters from these people to respond to, I wanted to identify these people and send a brief message.

1. **Tom DeMatteo** of Columbus, Ohio
2. **Wanda Tallhame** of Grafton, Ohio
3. **Diana Adelizzi** of Ocean View New Jersey

I have no doubt the letters you sent were as genuine and supportive as all of the others. I can claim with certainty that I read your letters, they just never made it back into the envelope. There could be many explanations as to the disposition of your letters to include they were washed away in one of the flash floods (Yes, there are flash floods in the desert) or possibly is now in the hands of another service member who appreciated them as much as I did. In any case, I thank all of you from the bottom of my heart for your efforts---your words and time were not wasted!!

CHAPTER 4

CHILDRENS' WISDOM & INNOCENCE

Some of the most poignant correspondence was written by children. The innocence and naivety of children always had a striking impact on me and many others. The following letters, cards and pictures were sent by children from around the United States. Some children managed to evoke some tears and others, a hearty laugh, while others simply melted my heart with their authenticity and unbridled honesty. Many of the children are affiliated with the Brownies, the Girl Scouts, and other significant organizations. While I reveal each of these letters, I secretly hope that some of these kids, now adults, recognize their work and that they reach out to me. Additionally, I hope that the candid revelations of each of these children resonates with all of you readers.

The USA is Really Proud of you!

We Thank you!

Please Come Back Safely. God Loves Y

BE STRONG AND OF GOOD COURAGE, DO NOT FEAR NOR BE AFRAID OF THEM; FOR THE LORD YOUR GOD, HE IS THE ONE WHO GOES WITH YOU. HE WILL NOT LEAVE YOU NOR FORSAKE YOU. DEU. 31:6

Dear Melissa Douzet,

Wow, you are so creative. I especially like the funny looking purple snake covered with hearts. Thanks for your encouraging message and the scripture---a copy of PSALM 91---which reminded me how fortunate we all are that God looks over each and every one of us. Your letter couldn't have come at a better time since I needed to be reminded. Your timing was impeccable! Thank you and be safe!

SSG. David Brown

ANY SERVICE MEMBER

Dear American Soldier,

Hello: My Name is Sally Byrom. I am 11 years old and I am scared. I never thougt I would live threw a war. I hope we live threw it. Your be really brave. I have watched T.V. on whats going on out there and I have prayed for all of you soldiers over there. My brother-in-law's brother is over there his name is [illegible] Jullette. Well I hope before the war gets any worse that Saddam Hussein backs out. He is crazy. I hope that this war don't last long it is very scary. I bet that you are really caring and willing and may God be with you and all the soldiers. You are in all my prayers.

PS Please write back if you can or have time.

P.s. I wear a yellow ribbon representing you soldiers in the Middle East.

Love,

Sally Byrom

Aubrey Texas
76227

Dear Sally,

I am proud to hear that you wore a yellow ribbon to support us troops. I would wear a yellow ribbon for all of you that write and support us if it didn't make me a visible target. You state that you are "Scared," but do not be since we are in Iraq to ease any fears of our friends and family. Your parents, teachers, and friends will keep you safe. You are so right about Saddam Hussein being crazy, but we will take care of him, I promise. You prayed for me way back then during the war and now you are in my prayers today. You don't know how much I cherished your letter. Thank you!

Your friend,

SSG. David Brown

1-29-91

Dear Service person,

We are a brownie troop of girls who live in Leonard Michigan which is 45 miles North of Detroit. The girls are ranging in ages from 5 to 9 years old; That is why many of the letters are pictures with no letters. As A nation we Are Supporting all the troops in their efforts to Free Kuwait. If There are any needs that we can meet please let us know. For instance, if you know of someone who has no one to correspond with we would be happy to "adopt" that person. OR if you yourself need a little more cheer please write us and we will respond. Our prayers are with you.

Sincerely

Renee Nance

Leonard, MI 48367

Dear Brownie Troop Members, Alicia, & Renee Nance,

I was super-excited to receive your letter. I've never been to Leonard, Michigan, but have been to Detroit and Deerborn. I appreciate all of the beautiful art you included; however, I believe I lost much of it. I do have one picture from Alicia and I have placed the image below my response. You mention that you would like to "adopt" any soldier who has no one to correspond with. I will pass on this letter to others to see if they might want to correspond. I already I passed on many of the pictures to other soldiers who appreciated them. You all made me, and many others feel special, and I know it would have been a privilege to be part of your "Family." Thank you for the vote of confidence and for "adopting" all of us. A special thanks goes to Alicia for her art shown below. Thank all of you!

Your friend,

SSG. David Brown

Alicia,

Thanks for the creative and fantastic art!! I wonder if you still love the snow and if you still occasionally make snow angels. I hope you one day discover your work in my novel. Take care!

Hey Andrea and Brownie Troop 87,

Your card was very moving and thoughtful. I especially liked your message to, "Come-Home-Safely." The hearts were a nice addition. If you are friends with my sister-in-law, Sherry Kohl, you are friends with one very special person. Her husband, John, and her son Ryan mean a lot to me. I can't believe it is already Valentine's Day, but here we are anyway. That's amazing that you have the same birthdate as Saddam. On one end of the spectrum we have you, who I can tell is a special person, and the other end, we have one of the most evil people on earth. Your goodness easily offsets his evilness. I hope you have an outstanding birthday and had many enjoyable ones since.

Your Friend,

SSG. David Brown

Dear Serviceperson:

My name is Laura Esclamado and I'm in 7th grade at Hanson Middle School. I'm also a gymnast at Gym America – a 13 year-old level 6.

The reason I'm writing this letter is I want to say thank you for protecting our country and others' countries, too. The support back in the States is tremendous – we're behind you all the way.

I live in Ann Arbor, MI. It's really a college town. Most of the stores are based around the college kids. It's scary to think that soon these kids might be drafted or volunteer. The U.S. is never going to be the same.

I wish you the best of luck, but those are just words. You won't need luck to defeat Iraq and Saddam Hussein. You have America (and the rest of the world) behind you.

Yours,
Laura

Hi Laura!

You must be a very good gymnast to be a level 6 at the age of only thirteen. For the purposes of full disclosure, I do not know anything about the various levels of gymnasts, but I do know you must have graduated through the first five which is impressive in itself. In response to your, "Thank you," you have my, Your Welcome. In one way or another every person supports others whether they are aware of it or not. I am proud to support the United States and its people just as you and others have supported us soldiers. The weather must be pretty-nice there in Ann Arbor, Michigan this time of year. I bet the winters are full of fun. Thanks for wishing all of us luck in defeating Iraq. It's is good to know there are awesome people like you who support us and have our backs. Thanks!

Your Friend,

SSG. David Brown

Dear Service Member,   1-29-91

Hi, I'm Heather. I am a girl scout. I would like to tell you that I support the troops over there. Also, my dad is over there. I wish that Saddam Hussein would get out of Kuwait. I would like to hear from you soon. There was a candlelight vigil to support you guys men and women are over there. What is it like to be in a war? My add You will have to write to me in care of the troop leader at her address.

♥   Troop #3000

Heather L.

P.S. Happy   Troop Leader's
                              Address
Valentines
Day !!!

Dear Girl Scout Troop 3000 & Heather from of Farmington, Missouri,

Thanks for having our backs by supporting us. Heather, tell your dad I said thanks for serving. I am sure he is alright and will be home very soon. I don't know if I ever replied to you way back then, but I hope you get this reply and you decide to contact me to let me know how you and your family are doing since. By now, I am sure your dad has told you what is was like to be in a war, but just in case you are still curious, it stinks! I appreciate each and every one of you from Troop 3000. Take care of yourselves!

Happy Valentine's Day,

SSG. Brown

```
     DEAR SOLDIER,
I AM 11 YEARS OLD AND IN THE SIXTH GRADE.
I LIVE IN WALKERTOWN NORTH CAROLINA.
I KNOW A LOT OF PEOPLE WHO ARE VERY PROUD OF YOU SERVICEMEN.
I HAVE HEARD THAT WHEN SOMEONE GETS A CAN OF SARDINES THAT
YA'LL FIGHT OVER THEM. THANK YOU FOR FIGHTING IN THE WAR! I
NEVER THOUGHT THAT THERE WOULD EVER BE A WAR.
                    YOUR FRIEND,
                    JENNIFER BRYAN

     P.S. I HOPE YOU WIN THE WAR!
```

Writeback

Dear Jennifer,

It has been a trying day. Many bad things happened, but we are alright. I returned to have your letter on my sleeping bag. It was like I was destined to get it. Your message made a big impression on me and helped me to work through some things I hope to never experience again. You are right about the sardines, but you won't catch me fighting over them. I would have to be half starved before I ever ate sardines! I never thought I would be involved in a war and, like you, I hope there will never be another, but unfortunately, we humans seem to be very good at it. I thank you for your timely letter and wish you the best!

SSG. David Brown

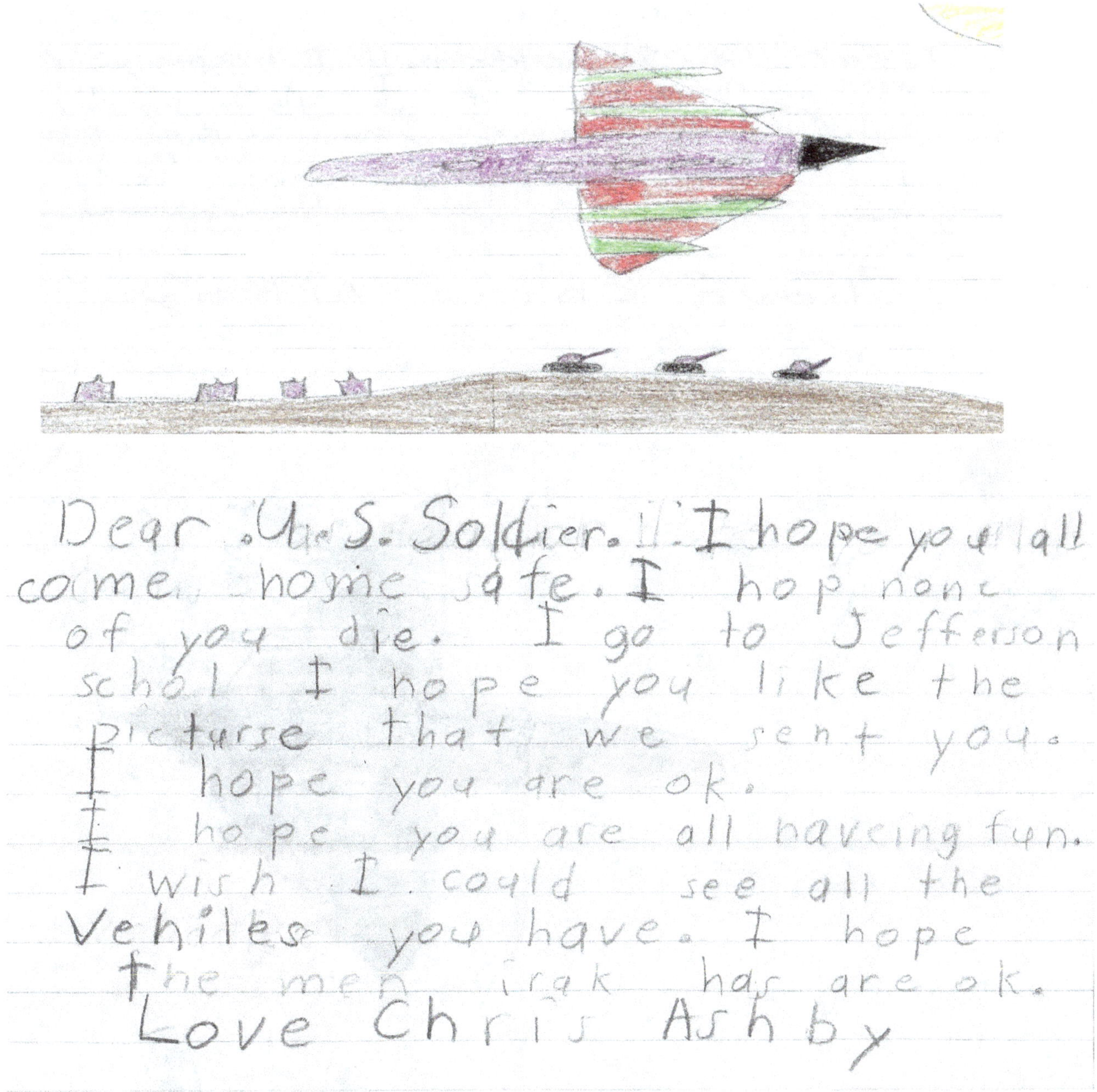

Dear .U. S. Soldier. I hope you all come home safe. I hop none of you die. I go to Jefferson school I hope you like the picturse that we sent you. I hope you are ok. I hope you are all haveing fun. I wish I could see all the Vehiles you have. I hope the men irak has are ok. Love Chris Ashby

How's it going Chris? Your Army pictures are impressive and yes, I loved them. I also hope none of us die, and we are doing our best to make sure that we live for a long time to come. We do manage to have some fun while here, but it's sometimes difficult. We support one another and joke around when we can. Thanks for coloring the nice pictures.

Your Friend,

SSG. David Brown

The picture that follows is from the same Brownie Troop from Leonard, Michigan that I recognized earlier. Apparently, I received more than one letter from the troop. The picture below is from Natalie and arrived with the same form letter as before, so I chose not to provide another image of the letter. Natalie, thank you. I bet you are a fantastic gymnast. I hope your life has been filled with happiness and joy since Desert Storm. I would love to hear from you one day if you ever come upon my book that documents all of the correspondence I received while in the Persian Gulf. Thank you!

Your Friend,

SSG. Brown

Nice touch here, Natalie!!

"ANY SERVICE MEMBER" MAIL

We were hopelessly lost in the Iraqi desert. My driver and I used a Cracker Jack compass to navigate. I am not exaggerating that is was a plastic kid's toy, but it worked perfectly and fastened to the dash of the 5-ton cargo truck we traveled in. Most officers and a few of the enlisted received GPS equipment that allowed for easy navigation, but we were not that fortunate. Navigating the desert is extremely difficult because there are very few distinct land features and simply getting back to the basics is not that reliable. Well, how about the sun rises in the east and sets in the west, some might ask? The truth is that this saying is technically not true since the sun only rises from true-east two to three times a year. At all other times, the sun rises from a slightly different trajectory. Besides, even if the sun consistently rose in the east, what does a person do when the sun is, for most of the day, directly overhead?

On this particular day we were on our way to repair a broken-down vehicle. Our compass was our guide and had never let us down over the past weeks, but today was a bit different. As our truck bounced through the sand, up and over sand dunes, our compass dislodged from the dash and fell through the hole around the gearshift. Piston and I looked at one another immediately as it plummeted out of the truck and into the dusty mise en scene. We searched for probably over an hour without any luck. In the end, we had no choice but to do our best to get back to our unit. We drove for hours, got helplessly lost, and at one point no longer knew if we were behind enemy lines or not. Keeping our fingers crossed, we eventually decided to drive towards the gunfire and prayed we ran into a friendly unit instead of the enemy. Luckily we ran into another American unit.

Our anxiety level was through the roof, when we finally reunited with our unit the next day. We slept very little since we were involved in skirmishes with the enemy throughout the night. I plopped down on my sleeping bag sending a plume of dust into the air. At the same time, a couple of letters fell to the ground. I excitedly picked them up, hoping that they were from family, but instead, both letters were addressed, "Any Service Member." I have to admit that I was disappointed, but still excited at the same time.

The first letter I opened was from Ms. Bonnie Larson from Thorp, Wisconsin. The very first line stated, "I appreciate and care about you…" Talk about perfect timing. Her words eased my nerves. She went on to declare God's plan to save us (A copy of Bonnie's full letter is below). The other letter was from Debbie Howie, twenty-four years old from Monroe, North Carolina. She just happened to be a huge sports fan and bragged on her favorite football team, the New York Giants who would be playing in the Super Bowl the day she wrote the letter. Her letter was just a nice, 'get to know you' style letter. The combination of both of these letters, I don't know exactly what it was about them, calmed me and eased my worry. The kind words of the thousands of people who sent letters to "Any Soldier" made the stress and fear found on the battlefield to be manageable. Sticking with Debbie's reference to football, the authors of each of the letters became the twelfth man on the field or in other words, they played a significant role in our success.

So, I would like to provide a special thank you to both Deborah Leigh Howie and Ms. Bonnie Larson for making such a significant impact on my life at a very trying time. Just months later, I received another letter from Debbie bragging on her Atlanta Braves and how they beat the then World Champion Cincinnati Reds 12-1. America is blessed with many amazing individuals!

Hello,   1-28-91

My name is Debbie Howie, and I am
from Monroe, N.C.
  I don't really know what to say in a
letter to someone I don't know, but
if you'll bear with me, I'll try to think
of something.
  I guess I can tell you a little bit about
me. My full name is Deborah Leigh Howie.
Everybody calls me Debbie, so please
feel free to do so yourself. I am 24 yrs.
old, 5'3", brown hair & eyes, and I
wear glasses. I like almost all sports,
especially baseball. My favorite team
is the Atlanta Braves. Somebody has to like them
My favorite football team is the N.Y. Giants,
who just happen to be playing in the
Super Bowl today. GO GIANTS!
  Well, what about you? I would love to
hear from you if you want to write
back and tell me about yourself, your
home town, your job over there in the
desert, or just anything you feel like
talking about.
  Well, I'm going to go now, but please
know that I love you, and am praying
for your safe return. Please take care.

                        Come home soon,

                            Debbie

Debbie Howie
Monroe, N.C. 28110

Dear Dave,   4-16-91 Tuesday

   Hi! I just recieved your letter
Friday, and I wanted to say thanks
for writing. I hope that all is going
well for you now.
   The weather here has been bad lately.
It seems like almost everyday the
clouds roll in after lunch and we have
one of those afternoon thunderstorms
that the south is famous for. And as
soon as it's over, the sun comes out
and stays out until dark. So at least
we know what to expect.
   I'm sure you must miss your family
terribly. I can't imagine being away
from my family for so long. I get
homesick even if I just go away for
a weekend. I guess it's a good thing I
never joined the Army, isn't it? I was
going to when I got out of high school,
but I was a little overweight, so I didn't.
Sometimes I wish I could have, and other
times I'm very glad I didn't.
   Oh, I just have to tell you about the
Braves game the other day. They beat
the world champion Cincinatti Reds 12-1!
It was fantastic! The Braves did pick up
a few good players this year. They got
Otis Nixon from Montreal, Sid Bream from
Pittsburgh, and Terry Pendleton from St. Louis.
So maybe they will have a chance to
win a few more this year.

   Well, I've got to get ready for work now,
so I'll go, but I do hope the rest of
your stay over there is safe, and that
you will soon get to come home. Please
take care!

                    Y'all come home soon now, hear!

                         Deidre

Dear Debbie,

I received two letters from you (Both above), one on January and one that arrived in April in response to a letter I sent you. In a different time and a different place you and I could have been good friends. I am a sports fanatic like you, but you will never catch me rooting for the New York Giants. I am with you on the Atlanta Braves though. I will root for the Braves over any team other than my Baltimore Orioles. After leaving the service, I ended up in Georgia and have since become a Braves fan (Second to my Orioles). You mentioned the "New" Brave's players: Otis Nixon, Sid Bream, and Terry Pendleton. Each of them in their own way helped the Braves rise to prominence in the 90's and they set the stage for Atlanta to remain dominant into the 21st Century. One of my all-time favorite players is Hank Aaron, so in a way, I was always a secret Brave's fan (At least whenever he played). You mentioned at the end of your second letter that you had to leave because you were getting ready for work. I have always been curious---where did you work in 1991? I hope you find my novel one day, so that you can fill me in. Thanks for your friendship!!

Sincerely,

SSG. David Brown

1/30/91

Dear Soldier,

I'm just writing to say I appreciate you and care about you and I mean all of you. Everyone that I've talked to cares and many are praying for you. I am, every day. Remember God is in control (our God, Jesus Christ) of all things. He promises if we trust Him Ro. 10:9 & 10 we will be saved. I hope you will. We care about you.

God Bless you.

Ms. Bonnie Larson

Thorp, Wi. 54771 USA

Dear Bonnie,

Your letter was perfectly timed. I just returned after another long night of stressful events and discovered your letter after laying down. Apparently, somebody knew I loved receiving letters and thought enough to place yours and one other with my things. I sincerely thank you for your prayers and for your guidance. It is sometimes so difficult to have faith that someone else is in control especially with all of the violence going on around us. Even in the midst of the chaos, while I sometimes have doubts, I do believe. Thanks for caring about all of us!

Sincerely,

David Brown

My thoughts
were with you
today...

Hi!

My name is Claudia Melaragni and I am a senior at Boston University.

I want to say thank you to you for your bravery and to let you know how much I support you, as well as the rest of our country.

I'm originally from Philadelphia, PA and will graduate from Boston University on May 12th with a B.A. in Biology. In a year's time I'll be applying to Medical Schools.

...and as a special way of caring I donated blood through the American Red Cross.

My thoughts are with you always.

If you want to write Claudia Melaragni

Brookline MA 02446

With my respect,

Claudia Melaragni

Hello Claudia from the Desert of Iraq!

First, you're welcome---in reply to your "thank you." By now you have long since graduated from Boston University, hopefully went on to complete med school and are now a doctor. Did you end up going to Med. School and if so, what is your specialty? If you chose another career path, I wonder what that might have been. You mentioned that you are originally from Philadelphia. I have been to Philadelphia a few times, and I graduated from Pocono Mountain High School in Swiftwater, Pennsylvania in 1983. Who knows, maybe one day you will find this response and respond to my questions. In any case, I hope you have had a gratifying, happy life. I would love to hear from you one day. Thanks for all of your support during those trying times. I appreciated every word you and others wrote. The victory in Iraq was everyone's victory!

Sincerely,

Staff Sergeant David Brown

15 May 91

To Any Service Member
Operation Desert Storm
FPO NY 09866-0006

© USPS 1991

Dear Warrior,

Thank you for defending my right to sit at home & raise my 4 kids. Thank you for standing up for our country! My kids and I (and our church) are praying for YOU. May the Lord bless you & keep you and save your soul. "Believe on the Lord Jesus Christ and thou shalt be saved." Acts 16:31

In Christ

Wendy Brown & Sarah, Jana, Laura & Noah

Well, good morning from Iraq, Mr. Jeffry L., Wendy Brown, & kids!

My reply has been a long time coming. I am sure I have an excuse of some sort. Let's see, if I remember right, I was in the midst of digging a foxhole or was on guard duty at the time. Seriously, I have no idea if I ever wrote you back and if I didn't, the reason was probably a significant one. I am from Ohio originally, but I am unfamiliar with Miamisburg. You will have to let me know where it is located in Ohio. I see you have four kids. Tell all of them---Sarah, Jana, Laura, and Noah, I send them a hearty, "Thank you." Please pass the message on to your church as well. I have two children, my son David and my daughter Ashleigh. Thank you for your prayers and positive thoughts. Take care of your family!

Your Friend,

SSG. David Brown

A special note: George & Barbara (letter below)
are World War II children. The greatest generation ever!

George and Barbara Jordan

East Greenwich, Rhode Island

February 1, 1991

Dear Service Member

Greetings from two people who are very proud of you and the job you are all doing over there in Iraq.

By the return address you know that we are from Rhode Island. My husband is a retired career Army Veteran and I am in accounting at a chemical plant. I am also proud to say I was a military wife. As I am proud of the part you are taking in this action, I felt this same pride for my own serviceman. It takes a very brave man or woman to fight for their country and their beliefs in a foreign country not knowing what price that stance will extract from them .

I am sorry to say this is not a personal letter as we do not know you nor do you know us but the feelings enclosed in these lines could not be more sincerely or warmer sent were they being sent to a daughter or son of our own.

We want so very much to convey to you the great support, pride and care your fellow Americans extend to you from small rural towns, villages and cities. From young children to older Americans as well.

We wish you could ride down country roads and city avenues alike and see yellow bows and ribbons tied onto lamp posts, front doors, bushes and trees. I drove by a school and the windows were covered with yellow ribbons the children had cut out of construction paper and attached them to the windows of their classrooms. Flags are flying to show the pride we all have in you and our country. It would please me if I could walk with you down the corridors of the building in which I work and show you again the many personal expressions of support which people from individual offices have displayed by and on their doors sending a message to all with eyes to see that they are behind you and their country from the start to a victorious finish of this war.

The night President Bush gave his State of The Nation speech the House and Senate gave you and your fellow service people a standing ovation with applaud going now for quite some time.

Not every person (for reasons of their own) wanted this war to start, myself included. You need only to look into a mirror to see my reason for hesitation. Be you a woman or a man, you are too special a person to be placed in danger if we could get Hussein out of Kuwait any other way. I am forced to admit now that I realize now it was only wishful thinking and not clever thinking my part. My husband counciled me that he would not leave Kuwait regardless of who ask him to. This man is beyond my understanding. His actions to this point leaves me with one desire, and that is to see his hide pinned to the barn door. If he felt he would break American's resolve by his hideous acts of aggressions he has made a grave error in judgement as people I have spoken with feel he has accomplished just the opposite result. People who would have preferred to go into this situation slower now want to see an end to Saddam Hussein once and for all. I doubt if many people will trust him to just promise to leave Kuwait. I know we wouldn't. Not now.

We are both pleased that President Bush did not pause as was suggested by some people in our own country as well as other countries, as we feel once we started to bomb and do away with this vicious man's defenses, we should not let up a bit and give him a chance to pull some other act of transgression while we were trying to attain a peaceful end to this war. We feel it would have been a very big mistake on our government's part.

I have not seen this country so united behind one goal since World War II. I was a small child
then but we all young and old supported our service people in anyway we could. School children proudly
lined up at the teacher's desk to buy Defense Bonds with our change. Adults recycled any materials
that could be used in the war effort. My job was to crush tin cans, scrap bacon fat and other solid fats
into storage containers which we turned in and to smooth out and separate the foil on my Dad's cigarette
packs. Mom along with other ladies and older men were active in Civil Defense working out of the town hall.
Our home was on a major highway and it was very common for members of the military to stop at our home to ask
directions to the Quonset Point Naval Station or to the city where they were making connections for other
points. Many of which Dad asked in and they ended up around our kitchen table having coffee or a meal before
continued on their journey most likely to a war being fought far away, never to be heard of again by my family,
but prehaps these young men were warmed a little by the few precious moments not only by the food or drink but
more importantly by sharing in a family situation even for a short time when they were so very far away from
their own homes and families. I feel my family wanted to share whatever we had with these young men because
they owed these brief guests so very much. Even as young as I was I can remember the good feeling we had if we
were able to lift a burden from a young serviceman even in our small way. This is the spirit I see now.

I am aware you have seen a few demonstrations of Anti-War groups. I have no real qualms with people
who are against war because I doubt if there are many people in stable mental condition other than Hussein
who feels that placing people's lives in danger without just cause is a desirable activity. However, flag
burners are extremely unpopular in this country. Please do not concern yourselves with these people, as
these very ones that are burning our nation's flag are in truth being untruthful to themselves. They contend
that they have a constitutional right to burn the flag but in turn they wrap the flag around themselves
and claim every right that was fought for and won by the best and bravest throughout the centuries like yourself
These people are not anti-war, they are gutless creatures. They have proved this themselves by the fact
that they are suddenly conspicuously not visible as they are aware it is not the wisest act to burn
the same flag that men and women are fighting under be it in planes, in trenches, in field hospitals,
supply depots, mechanical teams or whatever other source of support teams it takes to fight and win a war.
You continue to do your job in the fine professional manner which you have from the start and we will deal
with the flag burners. And above all remember that in comparsion to your supportors these gutless wonders
are very few indeed. They wanted recognition but now I believe most of them are hidding under their beds for
fear that some proud US Citizen from a nursing home will come out and beat them senseless.

We both hope by reading this letter, we have been able to convey to you the pride we have in you
and the gratitude we send to you, the few and the best for the job you are doing in our behalf.

May God Bless You and Protect You throughout this war.

Sincerely warm regards from two very grateful fellow US Citizens.

George + Barbara Jordan

Dear George and Barbara,

You are the first family from Rhode Island to send me a letter. Please tell your husband, thanks for his service. I
would love to hear his stories about his experiences while he was in the service. Being a military wife is like being
in the military, so in my eyes Barbara, you are a veteran as well. Thanks for letting me know about the support
from around the country. Reading all of the comments of support and praise are re-energizing. Thanks! I felt the
warmth of your message throughout your letter. You made me feel like part of the family. I would love to be able
to "Ride down [the] country roads and city avenues" to see the yellow ribbons and flags flying high. It must have
been an incredible sight. I can picture the scene in my mind as I read.

You are not the only one who was opposed to this war. I have received many letters with similar messages. I
personally thought it was the right thing to do at the time, but what is amazing to me is that while many have
differing ideas about the conflict, there seems to be an almost universal support of the troops. I heard there are
some protests and that is what is great about our country---we unlike many nations---have the ability to protest
and freely communicate our feelings.

I too am impressed by and proud of President Bush's resolve and determination to see this through. The Kuwaiti people needed our help. Like you said, Saddam was not going to leave peacefully, leaving only one way to get him to comply---force. It is tragic that any lives must be lost in accomplishing our goal, but on the other hand, hundreds of thousands are being saved through the efforts of our military. We all knew the risks when we entered the service and I, for one, while I do not want to die, would die content if I were killed helping the innocent rid themselves of a tyrannical murderer.

No, I have not seen any news of the protests, just what the people have informed me in letters like yours. We have been deep in the desert for months---no T.V. or radio here! Thanks for keeping me informed.

The efforts you made as a child during World War II, gathering steel to support war efforts and service in the Civil Defense is amazing. The whole World War I and II generation are to be looked up to and admired. I doubt there will ever be a greater generation of people! Thank you very much for writing. I hope to hear from you again soon.

Your Friend,

SSG. David Brown

Our thoughts and prayers are with
you all. May you come home
safe and sound and soon

Our best wishes

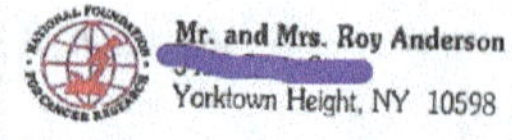

Dear Mr. & Mrs. Roy Anderson,

Thanks for the card. The strawberries make me think of Strawberry ice cream which there is none here but is one of my favorites. Thank you for your thoughts and prayers. I hope you are doing well in New York!

SSG. David Brown

January 31, 1991

Dear Service Member,

I would like to start by saying that I support what you and the rest of the troops are doing. You are brave people. Without people like you to fight for freedom, our lives here would be almost unliveable. May God Keep and protect you all. God's hand is upon this war. I am sad however, that any lives have been lost. Ever since Desert Sheild began, I have had a deep commpasion in my heart for everyone in our armed forces. I have friends that have been sent over there to fight in this war. One of these friends, has not contacted me. I have thought about him so much. I miss him. I know the chances of you knowing him are almost none. But if you by chance do, please tell him to write me. His name is Michael T. Stafford. He is in the Air Force. His hometown is Concord, N.C. He was stationed in England about a year ago. We met before he went. When he came home, we saw each other often. He is a good friend.

I watch the news every day to keep up with what is going on. I pray for all of you. I pray that God's will be done by our president.

I am a 30 year old, single parent. My son is 9. We live in a small town. Write to me soon. I would love to hear from you.

Sincerely,

Donna Lee

Hi Donna!

Thanks for your support. I'm sorry you haven't heard from your friend, Michael Stanton yet. Unfortunately, I do not know him. I have not seen any Air Force soldiers at all, after all, what would the Air Force be doing in the middle of the desert! I am sure he is alright and hope he reaches out soon. If he is anything like us, he is very busy. How are things going in New York? I hope well. Tell your son I said, "Hello." Take care of yourself. Thanks for writing.

Sincerely,

SSG. David Brown

This is Hilary

Dear Hilary,

Thanks for the bookmark, newspaper clipping, and the nice letter! How do you like Pioneer Middle School? Tell your sister, Melissa I said, "Hi." Thanks for taking the time to write while with your Faith Presbyterian Church Sunday School group. The war is all over the news, but don't be upset. We will take care of things here---you just worry about taking care of things at school and church. So, please don't cry. Thanks for the letter and for your support. Take care of yourself!

Your Friend,

SSG. David Brown

Feb. 3, 1991

Dear Service Member,

My name is Hilary Anderson. I'm a 6th grade student at Pioneer Middle School. I have one sister named Melissa.

I am writing this letter with my Sunday School class at Faith Presbyterian Church. I have heard about the war on the news, and I'm very upset. I cry every time I start thinking about it. We're all supporting and praying for you here. God will be with you all, because he loves you.

Sincerely,
Hilary Anderson

Life is fragile…
handle with prayer.

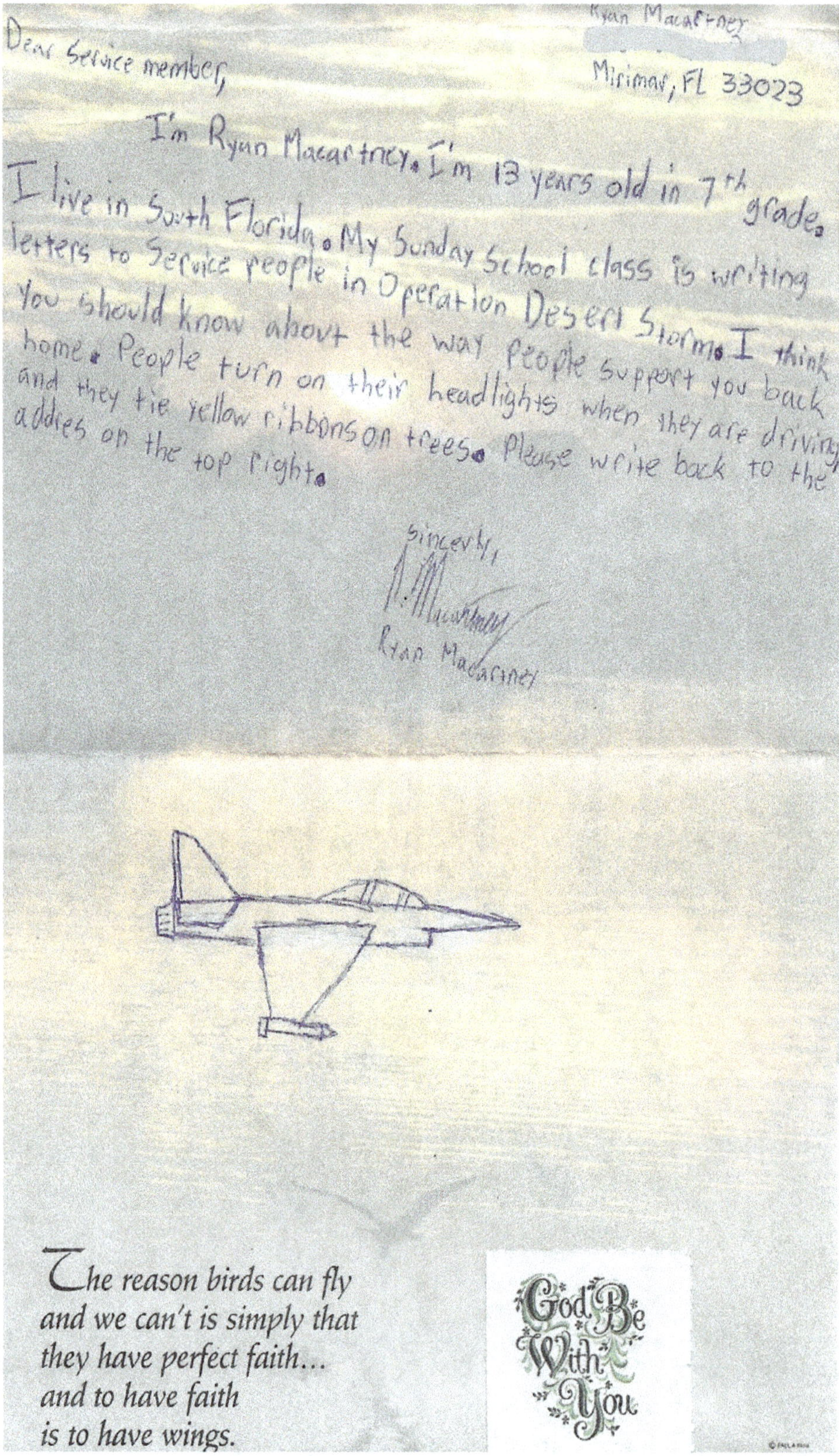

Ryan Macartney
Miramar, FL 33023

Dear Service member,

I'm Ryan Macartney. I'm 13 years old in 7th grade. I live in South Florida. My Sunday School class is writing letters to Service people in Operation Desert Storm. I think you should know about the way people support you back home. People turn on their headlights when they are driving and they tie yellow ribbons on trees. Please write back to the address on the top right.

Sincerly,
Ryan Macartney

The reason birds can fly
and we can't is simply that
they have perfect faith…
and to have faith
is to have wings.

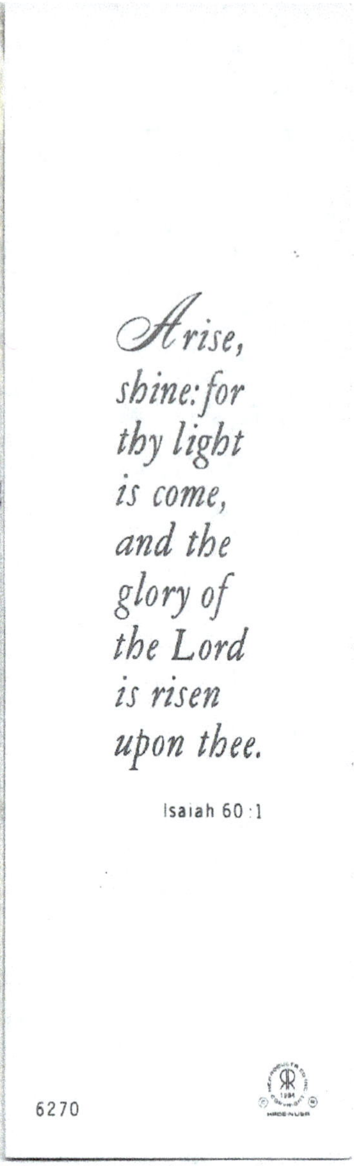

Arise,
shine: for
thy light
is come,
and the
glory of
the Lord
is risen
upon thee.

Isaiah 60 :1

6270

RO-AMERICAN RALLY: Luis Torres, 8, of Miami Springs proudly waves an American flag at Bayfront Park in Miami. Hundreds partici-pated in the demonstration, and motorists honked their horns in sup-port as they passed.

C.W. GRIFFIN / Miami Herald Staff

This is Ryan

Dear Ryan,

I received a letter from your Sunday School friend, Hilary too! You guys are awesome! Thanks for the newspaper picture, the bookmark, and your picture. Now I know two people in your Sunday school group! Cool plane you drew on your letter---you must be an artist. I have trouble drawing a stickman! How do you like it there in Florida? Are you near the ocean? I might go on vacation there once this is all over with. I wanted to thank you for your support. It must be cool seeing all of the cars with their headlights on and seeing all of the yellow ribbons around town. I appreciate you Ryan. Like the sticker on your letter says, "God be With You!"

Your Friend,

SSG. David Brown

1-27-91

To whom it may concern,

My name is Brad Copeland. I live in Franklin Park, Illinois. It is a suburb of Chicago. I am a freshman in High School. I am really thankful for what you are doing.

As you might have heard, there are a lot of anti-war demonstrations going on. But that really makes me mad. I think they should be supporting you guys. I know I am. It is really nice to see yellow ribbons & flags every where you go. Even though I would like to see the war end as quickly as possible, I know you have a job to do & I know you will do it To the best of your ability. I get a good picture about what it is like to be over there, by watching T.V. I can imagine how boring it is over there. Like one reporter said, the highlights of the day are eating and reading your mail.

I would just like you to know that we are thinking about you, and praying that you will come back safely.

Your friend,
Brad Copeland

P.S. My address is on the back if you would like to wright back to me, I would like to here from you.

Dear Brad,

Boy, the freshman year in high school can be tough. I hope it goes well for you. I didn't hear anything about the anti-war demonstrations directly from the news since we don't get any news out here, but many people who have written have talked briefly about them. I know one thing, even if protests are going on, people like you who write and express their thankfulness means a lot. I hope the war ends quickly too, and I think it will. We haven't met with too much resistance other than a couple of days. We are expecting to be meeting up with stragglers from the remnants of the Iraqi Army at this point and that should be it. Yes, there can be some boring days, but we are on our toes. We are not in the rear like that reporter, but instead we are always on the front lines and have to be alert. I don't see any reporters up here nor do I expect to, so, yes, he is probably bored sitting on his butt waiting for a story. I appreciate you taking the time to write and hope your first year of high school goes well. It's up to you to make it a memorable four years! Take care!

SSG. David Brown

CHAPTER 6

PATRIOTIC MESSAGES

Many strangers shared their thoughts, hopes, and best wishes through their letters. The messages included were universal. Letters arrived from all over the United States to include from Rhode Island, New York, Arizona, North Carolina, Utah, Florida, Illinois, Maine, Ohio, and every other state. No matter where the messages came from, the themes of each were similar: We support you, we hope all of you are alright, we hope you get home very soon, and we are all proud of you. What more could a soldier ask for than the support of her/his local community, state, and country.

Sometimes there might seem to be nothing good that comes from an event, especially war, but I submit that some good things came out of this war besides the obvious. Yes, we freed Kuwait and removed a despot from power, but war has other unexpected consequences. First, oftentimes, the stresses and responsibility of life in general tends to pull family apart. Family moves, career changes, differing values, and different choice of friends are just a few possible circumstances that have the possibility of driving a wedge between families.

Similarly, friendships can be ended by sometimes trivial things. Arguments about sexual partners, boyfriends, girlfriends, misunderstandings, and varying professional paths can all temporarily or in some cases, permanently dissolve long standing relationships. A friendship lost is a tragedy but mending them is remarkably satisfying.

War, while an insidious action, does have its ability to mend relationships and ultimately, brings people together. When people share similar experiences, the natural response is to unite as a team to overcome adversity. While it is disappointing that it takes tragedy to unite people, conflict(s) has this capability. Desert Storm, if only for a short time, united our country. Maybe someday our country will unite again for good.

Any service member,

Hello! My name is Cheryl Griggs. I am 18 yrs old. (Will be 19 on Feb. 9) I live in Stanley, N.C. I am in my first ~~year~~ year of college. I am attending a local college.

How long have you been in Saudi Arabia? What branch of the service are you in? I hope things are going good for you in S.A.

I know how your family feels about you being in S.A. My dad is in the national guard & he is in S.A. (the capital).

What kind of music do you listen? How old are you? How long

Have you been in the service? Where do you live? If you would like anything or need anything - let me know & I'll get it for you! Please tell me some things about yourself !?

I am going to go for now - I have to write to my dad! Be careful & may God Bless you.

Happy Valentines Day

Cheryl Griggs
Stanley, N.C.
28164

Dear Cheryl,

I hope college is going well. I took some classes at the University of Maryland European Campus and at Pierce County College in Washington State over the past few years. I had to withdraw from classes due to Desert Shield. I have been here about a month and a half so far, but it seems much longer. Things are going pretty well. I hope your dad is doing well. Make sure you write him often and he will be happy with that for now. To answer your questions, I like all kinds of music, but mainly rock. I am twenty-six years old. I have been in the Army for seven years at this point. I was stationed in Baumholder, Germany for the past 2-1/2 years before being deployed here. I am originally from Ohio, but have lived in Colorado, New Jersey, graduated high school in Pennsylvania, lived in Washington, and also Kentucky for a short time. I appreciate your offer to send things, but we are doing pretty well with all of the care packages that people have sent. You are very generous to offer. Thanks for taking time to write me. Happy Valentine's Day to you too!

SSG. David Brown

19 February 1991

My Dear Fellow American;

As I walk through my neighborhood or drive through our cities and towns I see American flags waving from porches and business places, and yellow ribbons tied to trees, fences and car aerials. Enclosed is a picture of my home in Magna, Utah.

Each day I listen to news broadcasts hoping to hear good news that this war is over, and each night I pray for your safety and that you will soon be home with your family and friends.

Of one thing I am sure, you and your fellow soldiers are doing what has to be done in order to save our world from being taken over by any dictator who has a mind to do so.

May God bless you in your valiant efforts.

Sincerely,

William Beck

Dear William,

Thanks for the picture. Many of the patriots who have written mention the yellow ribbons, flags, and other patriotic decorations around the various towns, but this is the first picture I have seen. Your house looks great! I shared this picture with my entire squad and more. I've never been to Utah but hope to make it there one day in the future. I believe the war is very close to ending. I am ready to get out of this overheated sandbox! It will be a wonderful day when Saddam is taken out of power and has to face the consequences of his actions. He is a true tyrant. I just hope our actions at this time serve to unite the Middle East and not destabilize the region. Anyway, thank for the great picture and your well wishes.

Your friend,

SSG. David Brown

4-17-91

Dave,
   Here's some things you might need.
If you don't need something, use it
as "collateral!"

       Your friend,
   Dave
        N Scituate, RI.

Dear Robert,

I never got your last name. This short note came with a large care package. I wanted you to know that we all enjoyed your gift and are indebted to you. Thanks!!

Dear Soldier,   2/8/91

I don't Know who you are, But I Wanted you to Know what a great job you, & everyone else out there are doing! Most of us back in the States are really proud of all of you over in the Gulf. I don't Know how long this letter will take to get over there, but I hope you get it before the end of the month! I've got two friends over in Saudi Arabia right now, but I can't get a hold of them. Gee, you guys must be ready to get back to the States, especially with all that sand you'r in now?? Have you been in any action yet? Well, I guess I'd better close, thanks once again for all that you'r doing over there! Hope this war dosn't last to long!

Sincerely,
Natalie Williams

P.S. Is the food any good over there???

If you want to write

Natalie Williams

Leicester N.C.
28748

Dear Natalie,

Thanks for the letter and your show of support. Your letter took just over a month to arrive here in Iraq. It may have arrived in Kuwait much earlier but had to be trucked to us in Northern Iraq. The main thing is that it made it, and I so much appreciate you for it. I bet your two friends who are in the Persian Gulf are fine. I imagine that they are getting settled in and are busy with any number of things. You will hear from them eventually—don't worry! Your right, I am more than ready to get back home and yes; the sand makes it miserable! I imagine we have at least a few more months here. We were engaged over several days as the Iraqis exited Kuwait, but things have quieted for now. To answer your question, the food is terrible. We mainly eat MREs[1] and the little Middle Eastern food I have eaten is very bland and at times very spicy. Again, I hope your friends are alright. Take care!

Your Friend,

SSG. David Brown

---

1 Meals ready to Eat: Prepackaged, often dehydrated meals.

Dear Service Person,
Happy Valentines Day! Take good care of yourself. I'm sure that would be the best Valentine for your friends & family.

Mary Dupuis
Rye NY 10580
26 yrs old originally from Michigan. GO BLUE!

Dear Mary,

Thanks for the Valentine's card! I always had a thing for Minnie Mouse---how did you know? It was very thoughtful of you. This type of Valentine reminds me of being back in elementary and maybe middle school so many years ago. It was one of my favorite times. I always saved an extra special one for whatever girl I had a crush on at the time, but they never seemed too impressed. I guess they didn't enjoy getting Valentine's Day cards with GI Joes and Superheroes on them! I hope you had a fun Valentine's Day. Take care and thanks again for writing! I am also a huge Wolverines fan!! Go Blue!

Sincerely,

SSG. David Brown

David,

Hi, what's up? Not much here. Just getting ready for prom and graduation. By the way if I didn't tell you in my previous letter when I was graduating, how did you know. Do you have friends who got letters from kids in my class who said or what? I guess it doesn't matter you'll tell me anyway, <u>Won't You</u>. (Just Kidding)

I've never been over seas before but I do know military life. My dad's been in the army + then transfered to the Public Health branch of the Navy. He's an O-5 which is <u>I think</u> like a Lieutanent Colonel in the Army. I was born in Colorado + since have lived in Abordine, MD; Silversprings, MD; Gallup, NM; Long Beach, Calg (twice); Browning, Montana; Phoenix + ~~Glendal~~ Glendale, AZ; + Canada. I may only be 18 yr old but I've earned alot of moving in.

How are things going in the Middle East? Do you think you'll be coming home soon? I'm sure your family really misses you. I know if my fiancé were over there I'd really miss him. Just out of curiosity, how old are your children + there ~~names~~ names if you don't mind. I'd like to say hi to them personally in a letter if you don't mind. You know when I send you a letter I'll say hi to them.

Yes, you read it right. I'm getting

married. Not right away of course course
but if things work out I'll be a Mrs.
on June 23, 1992.
   You said that you instruct in the army.
What do you instruct? I'm into jet
planes. I did a research paper on stealth
aircraft. I have pictures of airplanes all
over my my walls.
   Well I have to go to choir now.
We're practicing for a concert this Thursday
at Landmark Jr. High. Sorry so short.
Hope to hear from you soon if you
have the time.

                    Later Dave,
                    Your Friend,
                    Cecily.

P.S. If you get your orders to go home
if you want you cant tell me so we
can stop writing & if you like we
can keep it up & you can give me
your home address. It's up to you.
I dont want to cause any problems.

Dear Cecily,

It was exciting to hear back from you. In regard to your graduation date, I just figured most graduations took place around that time. As far as I know, you are the only one from your school that I correspond with. I can understand you wanting to travel overseas but being overseas is a bit different. I suggest exploring all that America has to offer first and then think about going overseas for vacation. If you ever decide to go to Europe, I suggest Germany. The people are incredibly nice and the villages are beautiful.

You're right, if your dad is an 0-5 his rank is Lieutenant Colonel which is a hefty rank. I hope he is doing alright in the Navy. I also lived in Colorado for a while. I was stationed at Fort Carson, Colorado just outside of Colorado Springs. How did you like living at Aberdeen, Maryland? I went there for a leadership school not long before Operation Desert Shield began. You sure have been around the country. What was your favorite place to live?

Things are going well here. I expect to be here at least another couple of months. I do miss my family, but between my wife, her family members, and my family, I get a letter or two a week which is helpful. Occasionally we are transported to temporary phone stations and we get to call home. Tell your fiancé that I said hello!

Let me answer your questions. I am twenty-six years old. I am not an officer like your father. I am enlisted and my rank is E-6, Staff Sergeant. I am the motor sergeant and I'm in charge of a squad of seven others. I have two children, a boy and a girl who are both very young. I will let them know you said, Hi."

Well, congratulations on your engagement! I wish you the best. I would be there if I could, but I expect to be here in Iraq or Kuwait in June when you are getting married. You will have to let me know how things go. You said you will be a, "Mrs. On June 23, 1992." So what is your new last name? Just curious.

Yes, I was a training NCO while stationed at Fort Lewis, Washington. I held classes on just about any skill needed for a soldier to succeed. Basic first aid classes, classes on protecting yourself from chemical weapons, survival techniques, and I even arranged and managed gun ranges. It was a fantastic job, but it came with a lot of paperwork and added responsibility. I enjoyed it though.

You will have to send me a copy of your report on Stealth aircraft. I would love to read it. Send some pictures of the planes too. Have fun at choir! I will do my best to let you know when I get my orders if things aren't too hectic. I sure hope we can keep in touch. I consider you a friend and I would love to see how your life blossoms going forward. Take care of yourself, Cecily!!

Hope to hear back from you!

Dave

THE HOLIDAYS, TOPPS TRADING CARDS, & MAIL

Many large corporations and smaller companies stepped up in one way or another to support the troops. Some provided free products while others supported family members at home. One of the most enjoyable and creative things (to me) that any company did during Desert Storm was Topps---the popular trading card company---distributing packs of special "Desert Storm" baseball trading cards right around Christmas or New Year's (Hard to remember). Most received a pack or two per person but by the time the leftovers got to us in Iraq there were only a few packs left, so we shared with one another. The cards were embossed with a Gold Palm Tree stamp in the upper right hand corner (See the image below). The cards served as artifacts that documented the historical event, but more importantly, provided a nice change of pace that helped many get their mind off of the war if only for a few minutes. I for one, have a passion for card collecting that sprouted when I was a young child in the seventies. Topps was and still is the premiere brand to this day. Unfortunately, out of the few cards we were able to gather on the frontlines, many were ruined by the weather and due to the effects of constant movements. In any case, to this day I appreciate Topps for their generosity.

Specialist Toad, one of my squad members, managed to hold on to his cards for the entire campaign. I ended up with three cards that I no longer have. Toad was eventually medevacked home due to a mental breakdown. The pressure simply got to him and he lost touch with reality, but he held those cards in his hand up until he was evacuated. He cherished them.

I bring this up because, first. The moment stands out in my mind as one of the more enjoyable events while in the desert and second, when the packs of cards arrived, it seemed like a holiday. We spent many holidays in the deserts of Iraq, Saudi Arabia, and Kuwait to include, birthdays, Christmas, Valentine's Day and others. People were especially generous with their writing during the holidays; cards and letters poured in from around the world. I was fortunate to collect a number of letters and cards from these holidays. I have shared them below.

yh DAVID ! AND ALL OTHERS...

YOU GUYS DID ONE
HECK OF A JOB ! AND SO
QUICK ! EVERYONE HERE IS
SO PROUD OF YOU ALL.
YOU'RE ALL HEROES IN
THE U.S.A. Our prayers
are with you + you're
loved ones til youre
on home soil.
WE LOVE YA ALL !

Put on some green,
Put your worries away...
Put on a smile,
Have a wonderful day!

and hurry home
where ya belong !

Mike + Lezbie Meeks
(on Forest Pk Dr.)
N. Ridgeville)

Dear Mike and Lezlie Meihls,

Thanks for the St. Patrick's Day card. Believe it or not, your card was the only one I received recognizing St Patrick's Day. The image of the bear with a military helmet is a nice touch! The U.S. Military did a stellar job like you mentioned and thank goodness the hostilities ended so quickly. Thanks for your kind words. I hope to be getting home soon which for a while longer will be in Germany. Yes, I have seen enough green and camouflage colors for a lifetime. I will stop worrying once I get home, and I hope my smile returns shortly after. I have a lot to process. Thanks for the card and nice note!

With appreciation,

SSG. David Brown

Dear Denise from Worchester, Maine,

Thank you for the Christmas card. I really enjoyed the message. I wish you, "Joy and peace" for Christmas as well. I appreciate your thoughtfulness.

Sincerely,

SSG. David Brown

Dear R.C. Strong,

I no longer have the envelope for your card, so I don't know what church you referenced in your letter or where you are from. In either case, I enjoyed the thought and the poem as well. Have a fantastic Christmas and New Year!

SSG. David Brown

HAPPY
VALENTINE'S
DAY!

Jessie

Ambassador

© 1989 Binney & Smith Inc.

© HALLMARK CARDS, INC.
MADE IN U.S.A.

"He shall give his angels charge over thee,
to keep thee in all thy ways. They shall
bear thee up in their hands, lest thou dash
thy foot against a stone."
— Psalm 91:11-12

Jan. 29 - 1991
Surprise Az,

Hello U. S. Serviceman or woman,

Sitting here in my safe home I thank God there are people like you who are willing to fight for what he believes and the freedom we have here and take so much for granted. May this war be over soon so you can return home safely to your family and friends. Whom I am sure is worried sick about you.

I live in a R. V. Park about 20 miles from Luke Air Force Base here in Arizona. We

hear the jets above us all the time practicing
to make it perfect if they are ever needed.
I never minded the noise they make because
I know what they are doing is very necessary,
as we know now it is.

I am a displaced Wisconsinite who has
been here in Arizona 5½ years. It gets pretty
hot here in the summer. One day this past
summer it reached 123°, which was a little bit
too warm. I don't care too much for the summers
here, but, the winters sure beat Wisconsins. Although
most of my children and all my grand children are
there. So we don't get to see much of them.
Will pray for a speedy end to this war & the safe
return of everyone. Sincerely & Love
Shirley Clauss

Dear Shirley Clauss,

I was SURPRISED to get your letter from, "Surprise, Arizona---Get it? I know—sort of dorky. I am glad you are feeling safe at home because that is what the military tries to do---provide a sense of peace and comfort. We all have that common human fault of becoming too comfortable and occasionally taking things for granted. I have had plenty of time to reflect and see all that I have taken for granted both since and before I arrived in the Middle East.

My mom and dad live in an R.V. park like you. They live in Ohio. Living so close to Luke Air Force Base must allow you to see many of the fighter jets flying above. The Air Force has some of the best pilots in the world—you don't have to look far for proof of that---from what I understand, the news does a nice job of reporting how well the bombing runs have gone and highlighting the accuracy of their precision attacks. This war would have an unimaginable number of casualties if it wasn't for the Air Force. Our air superiority will end this war quickly in my opinion.

Oh yeah, thanks for the Valentine card---at least I found it on top of your letter when I received it. The card is from a child named Jessie (Pictured above your letter). If not from your child---thanks to whoever Jessie might be.

Wow, what an adjustment moving from Wisconsin to Arizona. The temperature change in itself will be a major adjustment. I guess you have adjusted after 5-1/2 years of living there in Surprise. Yes, 122 degrees is super-hot. I don't think we reached that temperature here yet. The temp is normally averaging around 110, but often goes into the mid to upper teens (115-119). The heat can be oppressive at times. You are probably used to the heat in Arizona by now. On the other end of the scale, I am sure you enjoy the winters more in Surprise. I lived most of my life in Ohio and we had some cold, snowy winters. While the snow is fun, it gets old when you are constantly shoveling driveways!

I appreciate your prayers and your call for a safe return. Thanks for writing!

SSG. David Brown

Dear Sir

You don't know me yet, but I use Q-link (a computer net for Commodore) a bit (big bills) and I saw a post that I could send letters "To Any Service Member", so this comes to you. I thought to myself, anyone who is over with our forces must be a good guy! So I fired up GEOS word processor and got off this letter.

Since we don't know each other very well I thought you wouldn't mind me including the Christmas Letter. It tells some about my wife and I and fills in some details, so I don't need to type them over again!

I was cooking dinner when the reporters in Baghdad announced the start of the Iraq War on CNN. I put in a tape and have continued taping for days, so if you want to see what you were in when you get back, give me a call. From what I heard, a ship does not receive that much outside news.

Its a little cold here as I type. Weather man says around 5 or 10 tonight. It snowed again yesterday. I said I'm willing to drive for several hours just to see the snow, if only when I get home there's none around the house! My wife does not agree. She wants the stuff. Oh well, that's a woman!

I can't tell you anything about the sports scene, I'm just not into that. I'm much more interested in Science Fiction. After years of reading everything I could find, watching all the SiFi movies and Dr Who, I'm finally ready to do some writing of my own. I drive people crazy criticizing the plot or something like that of a book they like or a movie so now I'm trying to stay quiet and just write a better one. It's not easy! My characters sound too flat and the plot is too slow, but I'll fix it. Oh yeah, the powers that be have started showing all the old Star Trek shows over, starting with the first one. The uniforms they had then were just sweatshirts. I am taping that, too. Where I'm getting all this tape, I don't know.

There are so many American flags flying around town that you'ed think it was the 4th of July! We're flying one on each of our car antennas. And there are yellow ribbons showing support also. Our best wishes are with you.

I'm going to stop now and get this off. When some more things happen I'll drop you another letter. If you have time hanging heavy on your hands, let me know how you're doing.

Yours truly,   Q-Link name – "Zardots"

Alan & Diane Paetzell

Pawcatuck, CT   06379

Merry Christmas To All!

(Ok, ok, so it's not Christmas any more. Would you give me a brake? I'm not a fast typer, so you get this.)

Greetings to all our **friends** and relatives this 1990 Christmas! This is The Christmas Letter! Many are the things that have happened this year. But first, for those with Old Timers Disease, let us remind you of last years highlights. On Sept. 30th 1989 we were married in the park in front of a big tree with geese singing in the sky overhead! We had waited long enough, it was time to be joined forever. Our honeymoon was in Puerta Vallarta, Mexico, a tropical paradise with room service over looking the ocean. Every moment of our lives has gone perfectly since then.

Diane was offered a position as Ultrasound Sonographer in and around New London, CT at a considerable increase of pay with no difficult lifting which had been giving her trouble on the last job. After some thinking we took a weekend trip up to that area and looked for a house. We made a list of all the things we wanted in our new home.

1. Off main road. 2. Not smack up against neighbors, in fact, not many neighbors at all. 3. Have a big deck. 4. Have a water view.(front on water?) 5. Some room for a garden. 6. Lots of windows/lots of light. 7. Nice looking place, one we would not mind having friends over to. 8. A fireplace.

Well, as the religious teacher and writer Richard Warnbrant said in one of his books, "God never answers our prayers. He gives more than we ask!" We found a house that had been completely rebuilt inside and out. It has three decks! and is beautifully set under the trees back from the road with at least an acre of land (in which we planted our garden!) The back of the house is at least twenty five feet from our own dock on the Wequetequock Cove, a finger of water that looks like a river coming from as far as you can see on the left and going out of sight to your right on out to the Long Island Sound. It's about one hundred feet to the other side where fields and trees finish our view! We got everything we wanted and more! Well, no fireplace. We'll live with that.

Another addition to our lives is this Commodore computer that this is written on. The thing can even correct Alans' spelling! That's smart!

We are having our families up for the holidays. The tree in our living room is eight feet tall and five foot around. Oh yea! Duchess, our West Highland White Terrier, says "Hi!" to all with a wig-wag of the tail and asks her usual question, Have you seen any of my treats?

Merry Christmas to everyone, everywhere! Let us hear what is new in **your** life. Happy New Years, too!

Love to all,
Alan & Diane & Duchess

Pawcatuck, CT 06379
USA

Dear Diane, Alan (Zardots), and Duchess,

First thanks for your Christmas letter with the family update. Congratulations on your marriage and for finding your new home in Connecticut. Also, congratulations on acquiring your new Commodore computer. It prints well! I hope your family to include your West Highland Terrier, Duchess, have a safe and joy filled Christmas and New Year.

Your first letter said that you use Q-Link, and I have no idea what that is. I appreciate you taking advantage of the, "Any Service Member" mail and sending your letters. Unlike you who was in your kitchen cooking dinner when you heard about the start of the war, I was at the Saudi---Iraqi border awaiting the orders. It was actually a relief to finally get the orders to breach the border. We had been waiting in the desert for several days. You mention sending copies of the recordings you have of the news footage and state, "I heard ships do not receive much outside news." I don't believe any of us get much news if in the desert. I am in the Army, so the closest I came to a ship was helping to unload equipment when it arrived in Saudi Arabia.

I am also a SCI-FI fan, but at the same time, I love sports, especially baseball and football. I think it's great you are going to start writing. I am conceptualizing a novel in all of my free time here and hope to one day publish. You will have to let me know when you publish your book. I was never a "Dr. Who" fan, but I am all about "Star Trek." I believe I have seen every episode more than once. So fellow Trekkie---"Live Long and Prosper" (I hope to as well). Where are Spock and Captain Kirk when you need them? I have to keep this letter top secret. My squad members wouldn't let me live it down if they found out I was a Trekkie!

It's nice to hear about the patriotic acts across the country. I bet it is amazing to drive around and see all of the American flags and yellow ribbons everywhere. Thanks for taking time to contact me, "Zardots."

A fellow Trekkie,

SSG. David Brown

Mixed amongst the hundreds of letters I saved while in the Persian Gulf, a few miscellaneous items showed up with no name or address. The first is the image of the heart above. It does say, "Happy Valentine's Day," but other than that, nothing. Whoever sent it, thank you for your consideration and for your artwork.

SSG. David Brown

Jan. 30, 1991

Dear Soldier

I am 8 years old. I am in
The second grade at John
school in chicago. We have
been talking about the
war in school
We do not want this war and
we do not want you to get
hurt. We want yo to come
home I am sorry this war
happemed Thankyou for
what yo are doing. today

Dear Jessie Rojas,

Thanks for the Valentine wishes. I hope you are well. I see that you attend the, Jahn School? Is that Jahn Elementary School or (I believe there is also) the Jahn Arts school? It's good that you have been talking about the war. We all want it to end quickly and also desire everyone gets home soon just like you express in your letter.

Pizza sounds good. Hey, how about sending me a slice? Well, you better check with mom first. Thanks for wishing me a Happy Valentine's Day. You definitely made mine much better!! Thanks for the cool picture, Jessie.

Your Friend,

SSG. David Brown

GO TROOPS!!
SENDING YOU
LOVE and HOPE

Dear Soldier,
I hope that you
come home soon!!
Were rooting for you!!
Heres a picture
Love
Meghann

HAPPY
VALENTINE'S
DAY!!
WISHING YOU
GOOD LUCK!!!
from
WETH, CT.

Dear Meghann (Weth, Connecticut),

What a cool card you crafted!! Thanks for your hopes and love. You don't know how much it means to me to know you are out there. Your picture of the bowl of fruit is so good, I tried to eat some of the grapes and an apple. I believe you are the first to send me something from the state of Connecticut. It's good to know people like you are rooting for us. You must have worked hard to design this card---you are very talented. I hope you are doing alright. I want you to know your card made my day and cheered me up.

Your Friend,

SSG. David Brown

CHAPTER 8

VALENTINES DAY, ART, & CARDS

We had just returned from a drive through Kuwait City. It's strange to travel through a country that is so different in their beliefs and their customs. All of the women wore tightly wound hijabs while the men seemed to be defeated as they walked with their heads hung low. In a way, I don't blame them since their country was taken over and occupied by another. I couldn't imagine what these people have been through. While I am sure they experienced some horrific events, they should be grateful they didn't get trapped on Highway 80 (Highway of Death). Men women and children's' bodies spackled the area just north of Kuwait City as evidence of the brutality of the Iraqi military. Further north on Highway 80 to include the southern portion of Highway 8 which goes into Basra and beyond, blown up equipment, and Iraqi bodies littered the highway. I believe the images of that highway following the decimation and what I still believe to be, the many Kuwaiti bodies that lined the southern end of Highway 80, will forever inhabit the chronicles as one of the most horrendous massacres in human history. The death and destruction was shocking beyond all description, but is forever etched into my being.

I remember as an adolescent watching war movies and studying the Civil War in high school. Some of the most popular sayings emerge from the darkness of war. General Sherman coined the saying, "War is hell." He couldn't be more right. The Highway of Death will forever stands as an image that demonstrates the hell of conflict.

Dear Rattana,

I no longer have the envelope to discover your last name or address, but thank you for the beautiful artwork. I just returned from a long mission and was feeling a little down when I returned just as mail was being delivered for the week. I grabbed one envelope and it was yours. I am so glad too because it is colorful and cheerful. Thanks for being my best friend. I hope you have a happy Valentine's Day!

Your Friend,

SSG. David Brown

Thank you for
doing such a great
job and making
this a better world
for me to live in.

We light candles
and pray for you
every Sunday
in church.

Come home safely
soon.

My grandmother
helped me write
this as my
writing isn't too
good yet.

Daniel Hoffman
age 9

My grandmother
helped me write
this as I can't
write yet.
Thank you for
making this a
better world for me
to live in.
We light a
candle and pray for
you every Sunday.
Do your job
well and come home
safely soon.

Patrick Hoffman
(P.J.)
age 3½

Dear Patrick (P.J.) and Daniel Hoffman (Trenton, New Jersey),

I received a Valentine's Day card from each of you. Thank you very much! I see that your grandmother helped both of you do the writing. Thanks, grandma! I appreciate your praise and I pray that what we are doing does make the world a better place like you mention. Time will tell. Tell your church congregation thank you for the prayers. I bet it is a sight to see all of the burning candles during services. I never received grandma's name, but thanks for your kind words and thoughts. I hope all of you had a magnificent Valentine's Day!!

Sincerely,

SSG. David Brown

Hello from Kuwait, Darcy,

How is college going at Kent State? I hope you are doing well. I have taken some college as I traveled the states and Europe. I attended the University of Maryland in Germany (Yes, at the time they had a division in Germany), Texas Tech University, Pierce County College in Washington, and Big Bend Community college in Washington. No degree, but hope one day to finish up. I wish you the best as you work towards your senior year!!

Thanks for the Valentine's card and for your prayers and praise. When you write back, you will have to let me know about how school is going. We are doing well since things are winding down. I can't wait to get home. Anyway, thank you for the card and for reaching out. Have a fun V-day.

Sincerely,

SSG. David Brown

Hey Risa,

I guess it would be hard to write to someone that you have no idea about. I have the advantage of knowing your name and in knowing that you were caring enough to send a stranger a Valentine's Day card. How are things in New York? Tell me a little about yourself when you write back. I am 26, from Ohio originally, have five brothers and one sister. I am currently married with two children and live in Germany. I too hope to get home very soon. Thanks for the card!

Take care!

SSG. David Brown

Hello from Colchester, Ct.
    Just a note to say
Hi & hope and pray
(every day) that you'll all
be home soon. If there
is something I can do
for you let me know.
Take care of yourself—
You're special !!.
            Love
        Mrs. Ann Smyk

Colchester, Ct 06415

Wishing you
love's special magic.

HAPPY VALENTINE'S DAY

from "Grandma"

Dear Mrs. Smyk (Grandma),

I got a couple of Valentine's Day cards a couple of days ago from two children and their grandmother did the writing in each card for the kids. She went by "Grandma" also. You wouldn't happen to have two grandchildren names Patrick and Daniel, would you? It would be amazing if you were the same person. Anyway, I am thankful to you for the card. I have a feeling that we will be heading home in the very near future (Thanks in part to your prayers). You are the special one, all of you that took time to write to a stranger in a foreign land are special!! Thank all of you. I liked your card. I hope the arrow that the bear is shooting is heading towards Iraq!! Take care of yourself.

Appreciatively,

SSG. David Brown

Dear Service Member,

We are a family here in Milwaukee, Wisconsin that wants to thank you for all you are doing for us. We fly our flag around the clock, have yellow ribbons out and everyone of us is wearing a flag pin with a yellow ribbon.

Our family consists of my 80 year old mother, my husband who works at the main post office as a distribution clerk, I'm a homemaker and our 20 year old daughter is a student at Alverno college majoring in English with minors in education and Business and Management.

We don't like war and want all our people home but we have to stop that mad man and want you to know we are thinking of you and praying for you and will only rest easy when all our people are home safe.

Love,
Judy

...and my heart remembers you!

Happy Valentine's Day

Joe, Judy and Jody Smith
and
Violet "Vi" Bogner

Hello Joe, Judy & Jody Smith and Violet "Vi" Bogner,

I thank you for the Valentine's Day card! I've never been to Milwaukee, but isn't that where the sitcom, "Laverne and Shirley" is set in. They worked at the Shotz brewery if I remember right. I wonder, is there really a Shotz Brewery in Milwaukee. At the beginning of the show they always sang a song that went something like this:

"Schlemiel! Schlimazel! Hasenpfeffer Incorporated!"

I apologize for digressing; I just was a huge fan of the show. Many people don't realize that the song that they sang at the beginning of every episode used these old Yiddish terms that mean something along the lines of a clumsy or unlucky person. I can't remember exactly. Anyway, I know there is much more to Milwaukee, but I immediately think of that show. It sounds like you have a wonderful family. Wow, your mom is eighty! I hope to live a long life once I leave here. Tell your mom I said, "Hello." So you are a homemaker which means you are the hardest working of the family! My mom was a homemaker as well with seven kids and she never got a break, so you have my admiration. I hope your daughter Vi is doing well at Alverno College. If I ever get back to college, I will also major in English since I love to write, and I could always use some help with grammar and punctuation!

I don't think you are alone in disliking war. I am right there with you and the more violence I see over here, the more I don't like it. At the same time, it is a sometimes-necessary action to stop despots and tyrants from hurting others. The world will be a better place without Saddam. I feel confident we will all be headed home within a few months (Fingers crossed). I hope you had a fantastic holiday!

Take care!

SSG. David Brown

P.S. I received two identical cards from you just a week apart. You were all very busy. Thank you!

THE HOLIDAYS, FAMILIES, & ANY SERVICE MEMBER MAIL

As I opened card after card during Christmas, Valentine's Day, and for my birthday, I often thought about the stark contrast. On one hand, we are in the midst of a war, killing and maiming going on and on the other, we are being blanketed by mail filled with love and admiration. It seems to me that love outweighs the hate in this world and if this were true, then why does war exist in the first place? Love should stifle any hatred.

My favorite thing to do when I get a break from the war is read and write. I always looked forward to mail of any kind. The encouragement, sentiments, and praises of the writers took sometimes horrid days and through their acts of love, oftentimes raised me from the depths to a place of a well-needed joy.

Being away from family is especially difficult during the holidays; however, without debate, I knew that the mail would eventually include cards and kind words from family and from what were at the time perfect strangers (Normally, weeks after the holiday). Those who took the time to put up yellow ribbons, fly the American flag, drive through neighborhoods honking their horns in recognition of the troops, and especially those who sent, "Any Service Member" letters, each and every one of you were just as instrumental in the victory in the Persian Gulf. As far as I am concerned, the victory in Iraq belonged to everyone. Thank you for being the "twelfth man or woman!!

2/91

Dear Friend,

I just wanted to let you know how proud I am, as well as the rest of America is, of you. Thank you so much for all you are doing.

I hope the war is over soon, and you will be able to return home to your family + friends. Be safe, and take care of yourself. If you feel like writing, my name is Ilena Sullivan, c/o Shadden, Arps

New York, NY 10022

No wonder
     this little kitten
Looks so proud
     and happy, too--
She's the one
     who gets to bring
This valentine to you!

HAPPY
VALENTINE'S DAY!

Love,
Ilena

Dear Gina,

Thanks for the Valentine wishes. I hope you enjoyed yours. Your name reminds me of one of my very best friends I had while attending Pocono Mountain High School in Swiftwater, Pennsylvania. Her name was Gina, and I lost touch with her once we graduated. I hope to one day track her down. Anyway, I like your name---it brings back fine memories. Thank you for your undeserved praises. We are simply doing our job to the best of our ability just like everyone does. I do hope this chapter of my military career ends sooner than later. I wonder what it is going to be like returning after so many months of being hyper-alert and on edge and then suddenly be thrust into a relative peace. I worry. At the same time, I can't wait to see my family and friends. I will be safe and do my best to take care. You do the same. Thanks for being caring enough to write and send this card.

Kind regards,

SSG. David Brown

...for a day full
of happiness!

Happy Valentine's Day

Best wishes,
Stella Peger

I am writing both to wish you a Happy
Valentine's Day and to tell you that my
family and I, as well as the great majority
of Americans, are thinking about you and
praying for your safe return. We thank you
for your bravery in defending the principles
of freedom and democracy, on which this country
is based.

My heart swells with pride when I drive
through my town and neighboring towns in
New Jersey. Thousands and thousands of trees
proudly display yellow ribbons in anticipation
of your return and many homes are proudly
displaying American flags. Also, many people
are wearing a symbolic yellow ribbon.

Our prayers are with you.

WIN IT FOR PEACE
AND RETURN HOME SAFELY!

Stella Peger

Dear Stella,

 "Stella! Stella!" Sorry I always wanted to yell that just like Marlon Brando does in the film, "A Streetcar Named Desire." It probably gets old for you. I apologize—just need a bit of comic relief— this is my poor attempt at humor.

Thank you for the letter and card. Thanks for your prayers for a safe return. I hope to be back within a few months. You mention how you were, "pleasantly surprised to see such a larger-than-usual attendance" at church. One of the toughest things for a leader to do in our country or any other is to bring people together. It's unfortunate that it often takes tragedy or in this case war for the unification of people to occur. My mom once told me that something good comes out of everything bad. This definitely holds true for war. Letter after letter I read tells how the country seems to be coming together. We humans are a funny species.

Please let everyone know at your church that we appreciate their prayers. While you say that your, "Heart swells with pride when you drive through town," likewise, my heart swells with pride as I read one inspirational letter after another. America is a genuinely great country. Thank you for the card and taking time to write.

Please! Indulge me just one more time---"Stella! Stella!"---Thanks for your patience!

Take care,

Staff Sergeant David Brown

Greetings from Boston!

Hope you are safe this Valentine's day. We here are very proud of what you are doing.

Everywhere people are flying flags and putting up yellow ribbons to show support. You can't buy yellow ribbon anywhere its all sold out!

My family and I pray for your safe return home to your family.

This nice bunny
is bringing you
A Valentine's Day "Hi"
Because today is special.
And you're special, too--
that's why!

HAPPY
VALENTINE'S DAY

Pat Murphy

Hello Pat!

How are things going in Boston? First, thank you for the Valentine Day card. It says here that you are a "Nice bunny." What a relief. We definitely don't need any more mean bunnies! I've heard about many of the amazing things going on around America. The yellow ribbons, flying of flags, and the patriotic acts of people are inspirational. How is the weather there in Boston this time of year? We are expecting flurries and about an inch of snow overnight. I'm sorry I thought I was back in Germany for a few minutes. No snow here! I am hoping so much to be home, I momentarily thought I was there. It was snowy when we left Baumholder, Germany so many months ago. I imagine you get a good share of snow in Maine. I've never been there, but my dad was from Maine and he swore it was the most beautiful state in the country.

Well thanks again for the card and your inspiring words.

Warm Regards,

SSG. David Brown

Happy Valentine's Day
where ever
you may be....

Dear Dave,

There couldn't be a better day
To stop and reminisce
About the happy times we've known
And people that we miss,
And so this comes across the miles
With special thoughts of you,
And with a wish for happiness
Today and all year through!

All our love, thoughts
and prayers,

Marty, Nancy
and
Marty III
Rafine

Dear Marty, Nancy, & Marty Junior,

Regards from Kuwait! Over the months we progressed through Saudi Arabia, into Iraq, and now we are in Kuwait. It's funny---they all look the same to me only the path of destruction has slowly dwindled in concert with our movements. Thanks for the nice card. Still hot as can be, but at least marginally safe. I know Susan must be in contact with all of you. Hopefully you have been able to see her and the kids. Thanks for staying in touch and for your support. Your thoughts mean more than you will ever know. I hope all of you had an enjoyable V-day. Take care for now and write again if you get the chance.

Love,

Dave

Dear David,

Let just start of telling you who I am and how I got you name and address. My name is Wanda Tallhamer and your mom sent me some labels with your name and address on them. I've know you mom fo about 5 years. When she was working for Home Health Aids in North Ridgeville She used to take care of my handicapped brother, and my family And you mother became great friends along with Bobby and Kim. Well a little about me and my family. Well I'm 17 years old I'll be 18 (Jan 31). I am a senior in high school, I'm attending Lorain County Joint Vocational School I'm studing to become a cosmetologist (a beautician). I live with both parents, and I have 2 older brothers and no sisters. I no very little about you because I've never met you yet. I'll continue to pray for you and all others over there. I have 2 cousins there also. So I pray every night so I'll add you name to the list of loved ones who's names I know and even though I don't know names I still pray.

Keep the faith in the Lord and I'll continue to pray.

Love Always
your friend and
playing partener

Wanda Tallhamar

P.S. I'll try to write when I can. I know the more letters from home towns the better because I know it helps keep down the loneliness of friends and family.

P.P.S. I hope to meet you and your family one day when you come to see your mom, dad, and family.

Dear Wanda,

Any friend of my mother is a friend of mine! I am glad you took the time to write. I am so glad that she was able to help your family and that you became good friends. I am not surprised because my mom had a knack of making friends very easily. It's also great that you were able to meet my brother Bobby and sister Kim.

So how do you enjoy attending (or not) Lorain County Joint Vocational School? I hope you become a great cosmetologist. Cosmetology is definitely a trade that you will always have employment and can pay well. Good luck!

 Thanks for adding me to your prayer list. Your cousins will be fine. We do a nice job of looking out for one another. If you speak or write to them, let them know Staff Sergeant Brown appreciates their efforts.

I would very much appreciate you writing when you can. You have no idea how much your letters help. I appreciate you taking the time to write. Take care and I hope school goes well. Let me know when you get the chance.

Your Friend,

SSG. David Brown

"PICTURES FROM THE PERSIAN GULF"

Top Photo: Apache Helicopter being loaded onto a military transport at the Port of Damman, Saudi Arabia.

Bottom Photo: Crane unloading an M35A2 deuce and a half cargo truck. Two, 2-1/2 ton cargo trucks sit already unloaded in the foreground.

A photo of Staff Sergeant Brown at the Port of Damman, Saudi Arabia with a large container ship in the background (awaiting unloading).

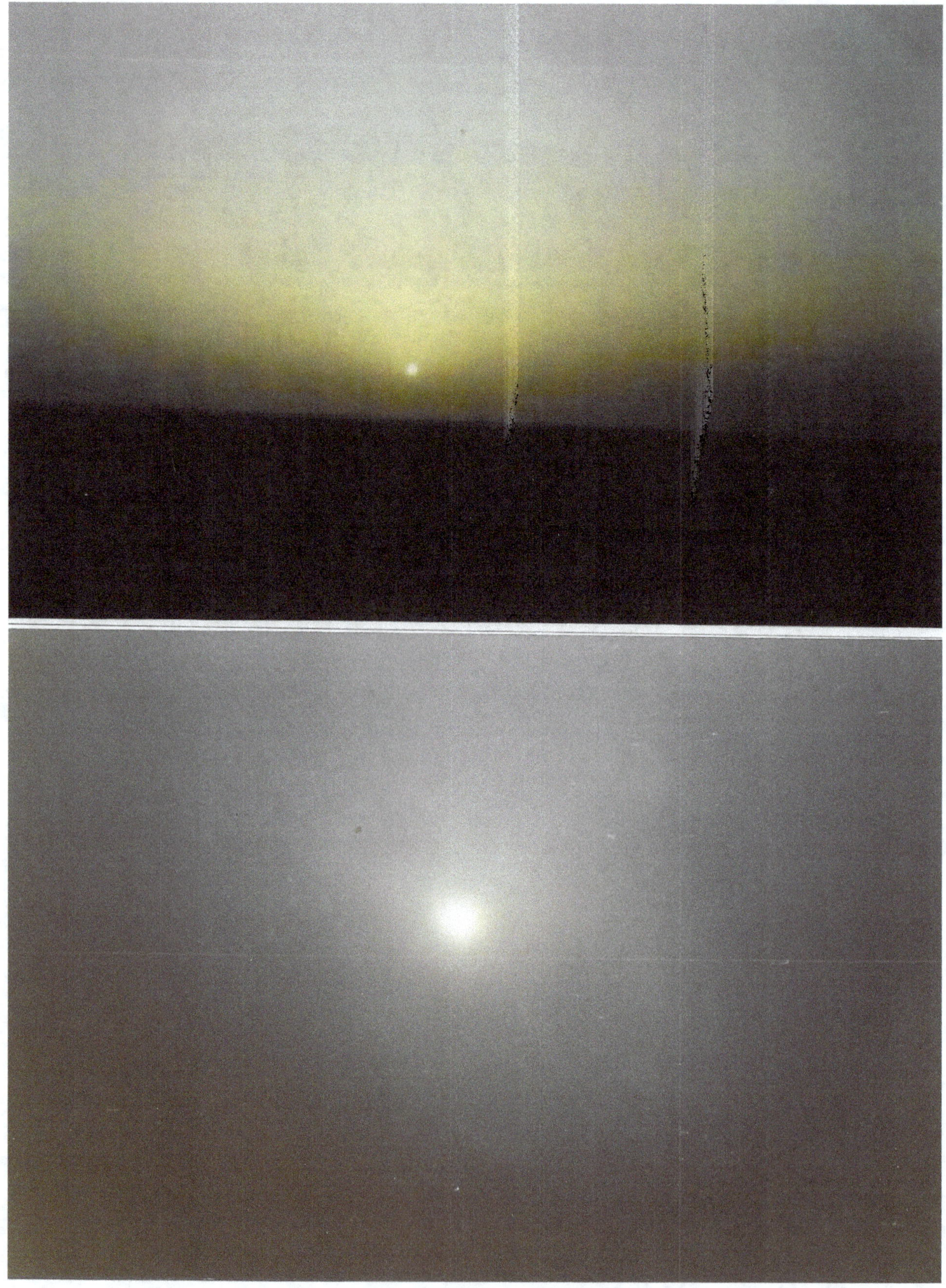

Pictures taken miles from the burning wells on the Iraqi-Kuwaiti border. These shots were taken during the middle of the day to highlight how thick the smoke was from the burning wells.

Top Picture: Sunrise in Kuwait blotted out by the smoke from the well-fires.

Bottom Picture: Various equipment at a rendezvous point. Notice the upside down "V" painted on each vehicle. All coalition forces had this mark on their equipment to identify them as friendly. Burning wells in the distance.

Both photos depict the burning wells on the Kuwaiti-Iraq border. Retreating Iraqi troops set the wells on fire in order to disrupt Kuwait's ability to recover economically and to hinder the rebuilding of infrastructure.

Top Picture: Taken in Iraq. The smoke had an impact even miles from the burning oil wells.

Bottom Picture: Photo taken in Iraq. Taken while I was in the midst of digging a foxhole.

Top Photo: M113 Track Personnel Carrier in operation during movements in Iraq.

Bottom Photo: Destroyed Russian-made T60 series tank following an evening of battle. The desert was riddled with disabled and destroyed Iraqi equipment.

Top Photo: A Russian-Made T50 or T60 Series tank. Our unit repaired this tank and drove it during our unit movements. I was informed that this tank eventually made it to a military museum on a base somewhere in Germany.

Bottom Photo: A couple of Russian-made Iraqi tanks destroyed during battle.

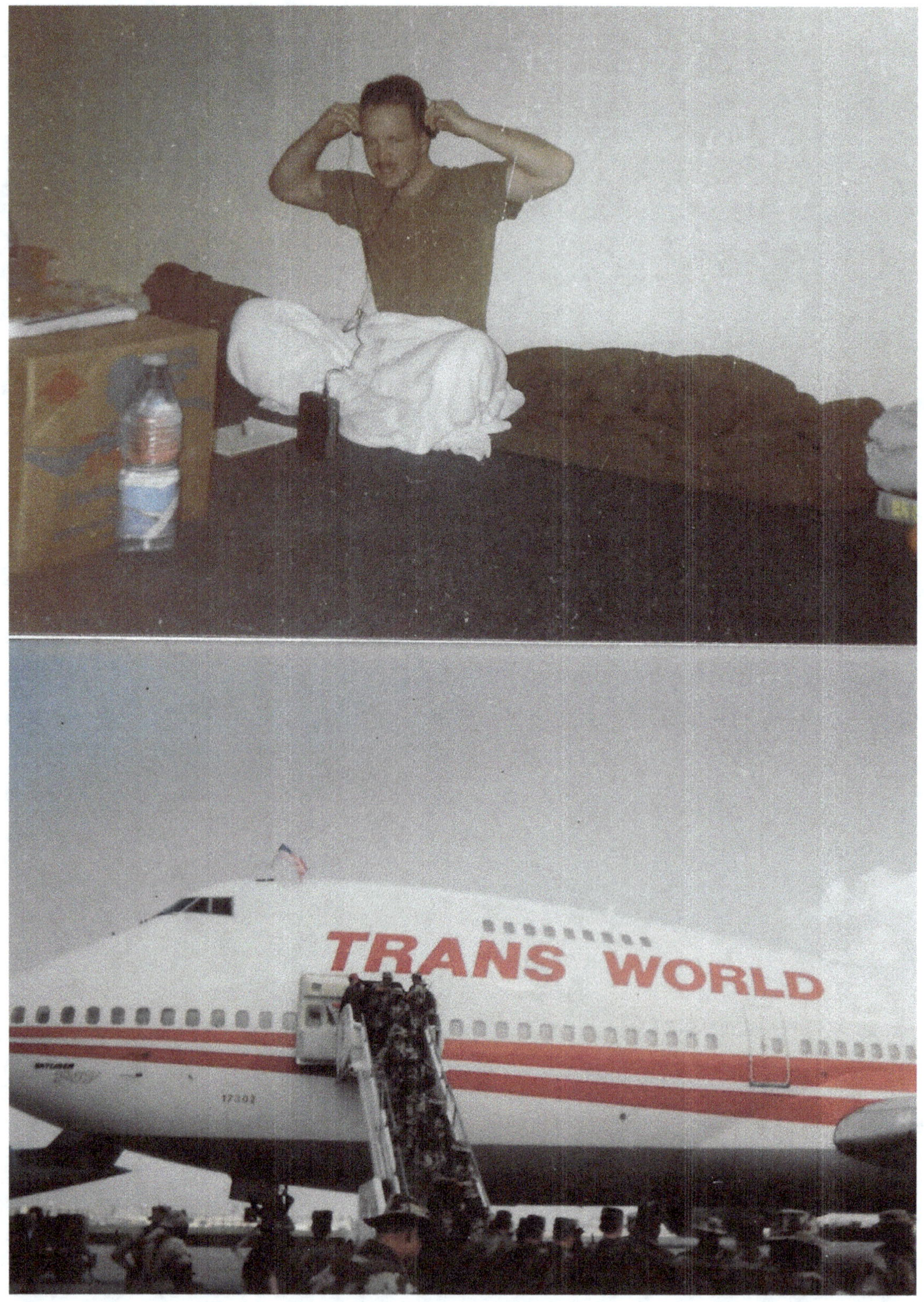

Top Photo: SSG. David Brown in a Saudi Arabian hotel prior to movement to the Port of Damman. Building was later hit by a SCUD missile.

Bottom Photo: My unit and others unloading after a long flight home to Ramstein Air Base, Germany following the war. I am the ninth from the bottom on the steps---(Honestly, I have no idea where I stood).

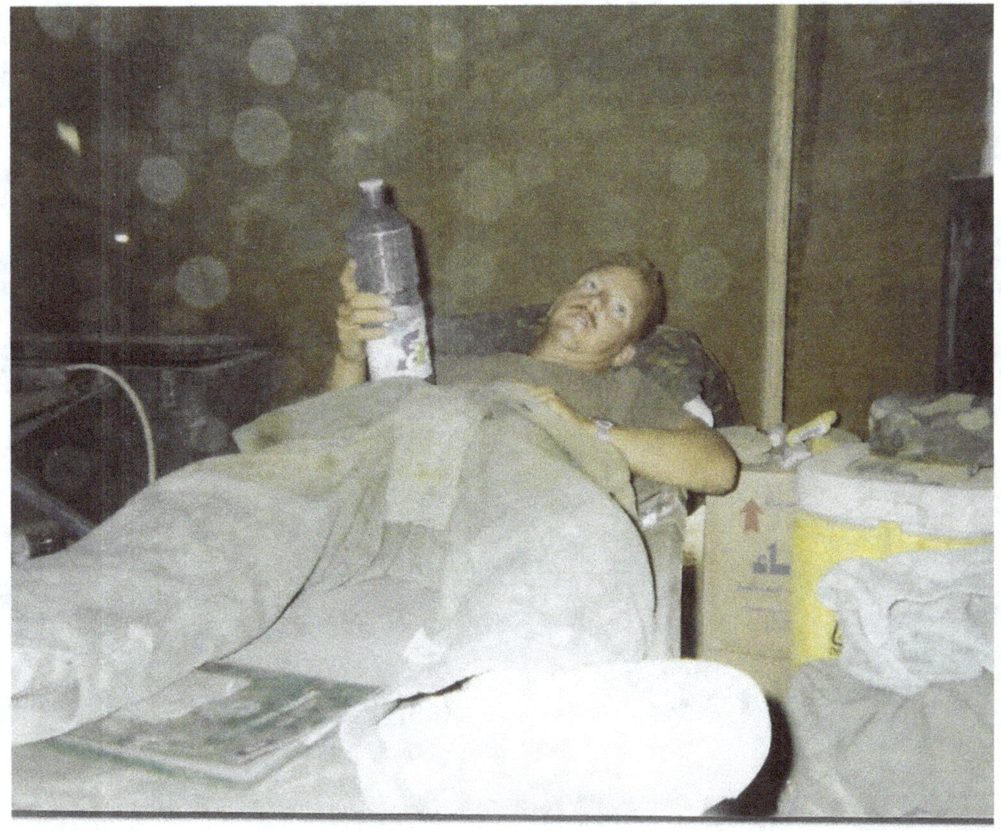

Top Photo: SSG. Brown after a long day's work following the war. Picture is taken in a tent-city located in Kuwait after the hostilities.

Bottom Photo: Name Tag and Branch of Service Tag from one of SSG. Brown's uniforms worn during Desert Storm.

Top Image: The two upper images are pictures of the shoulder boards that identify the rank of the wearer while in dress greens.

Bottom Image: Insignia patch for Army Forces Command worn on Camouflage Battle Dress Uniform.

Top Image: Two Eight Infantry Division patches worn on Battle Dress Uniform. I was part of the Eighth Infantry Division while stationed at Fort Carson, Colorado.

Bottom Image: Third Armored Division Spearhead patch. Unit we were attached to for a good bit of the war.

Under any circumstances, war is an unimaginable event that not only impacts members of the military, but also effects all aspects of society. Through no fault of their own, families and friends sometimes lose contact with their loved ones serving in far away lands especially during times of war. Likewise, soldiers serving in the combat zone, those fighting on the front lines, find communicating with loved ones and friends extremely difficult. Despite the companionship of their comrades, the lack of contact with family and friends abroad often leaves them feeling isolated and alone at a time when contact with the outside world is critical.

During war, soldiers look for anything that might provide even the most minute advantage. Things that build morale are especially valuable and sometimes serve as a motivational force that furnishes the little extra push needed to succeed on the battlefield. The letters included in this collection not only delivered the additional drive soldiers needed to prevail over the sometimes-extraordinary challenges of war but in many cases, propelled the military to victory.

The impact of patriotic Americans across the country who took the time to correspond each indirectly contributed to victory in the Persian Gulf. While the many authors who took the time to write will never receive credit for their contribution to the war effort, I hope the contents of this text brings a well-deserved credit to all of the writers who served as the twelfth man on the battlefields of Iraq and Kuwait. Your contributions were invaluable to the war effort and the subsequent victory. This epistolary novel serves as a tribute to each person who took the time to write, especially those whose letters, cards, and art are included in this collection of historical documents. Let this text serve as an overdue and well-deserved heart-felt, "Thank you," for your selfless acts of kindness and support during Operation Desert Shield and Desert Storm. I and so many others, are indebted to all of you for your generosity and the peace of mind your words provided each of us.

ABOUT THE AUTHOR

David Brown served in the United States Army earning the Bronze Star Award for his actions during Operation Desert Storm. After exiting the Army in 1992, he earned his Bachelor's Degree in English with a secondary certification in Special Education from the University of West Georgia and later earned his Master's Degree in English with a concentration in Creative Writing from Southern New Hampshire University. For the last eight years, he served as a Special Education English and Journalism teacher at the Haven Academy at Alexander Comprehensive High School in Douglasville, Georgia and additionally, spent the last four years as an adjunct professor at Georgia Highlands College teaching writing/composition. This is his fourth published work.